W9-BUP-433

SOCCER
fitness training

by

Enrico Arcelli and Ferretto Ferretti

Library of Congress Cataloging - in - Publication Data

SOCCER *fitness training*
 Arcelli, Enrico and Ferretti, Ferretto
Original Title "Calico: Preparazione atletica. La resetanza aerobica e
lattacida nel calcitore dilettante e professionista

ISBN No. 1-890946-21-4
Library of Congress Catalog card Number 98-67119
Copyright © February 1999

All rights reserved. Except for use in a review. The reproduction or utilization of this book in any form or by any electronic, mechanical, or other
means, now known or hereafter invented, including Xerography,
Photocopying and Recording, and in any information storage and
retrieval system, is forbidden without permission of the publisher.

Reedswain Books are available at special discounts for bulk purchase. For
details, contact Reedswain at 1-800-331-5191.

Photography (cover) EMPICS	*Art Direction, Design and Layout* Kimberly N. Bender
Graphic coordination S&A, Milan	*Editing and Proofing* Bryan R. Beaver
Editorial coordination Marco Marchei	*Printed by* DATA REPRODUCTIONS Auburn Hills, Michigan
Translated from Italian by Maura Modanesi	

REEDSWAIN BOOKS and VIDEOS
612 Pughtown Road
Spring City, Pennsylvania 19475 USA
1-800-331-5191 • www.reedswain.com

SOCCER
fitness training

by
Enrico Arcelli and Ferretto Ferretti

Published by
REEDSWAIN INC

Table of Contents

Introduction

In many Latin countries - among which Italy plays a role of critical importance - soccer is not only a typical custom, but also a sports discipline 'played' directly on the field, constantly 'discussed' and 'analyzed' both from the technical-tactical and biophysiological points of view. It is evident that any worthwhile technical movement cannot be prepared and successfully achieved without being perfectly supported by specific biochemical, biophysical and physiological research.

The reality of these important considerations was first developed and refined in highly professional circles and then gradually spread out to touch the whole of the soccer world, both at the professional and amateur levels. This inevitably led to the development of various technical and scientific soccer doctrines, which often contradict each other regarding empirical data and their interpretation. This clearly shows that Italian soccer is still living its successful years, characterized by 'the constant search for something new' with that great passion which has now become an out-of-date reality both on and off training and match fields in other old disciplines like track and field.

Although it is difficult to draw definite and final conclusions even for the most prepared experts of technical and biological disciplines, today all the people working in soccer must clearly know all the various physiological mechanisms involved in the technical performance characterizing the soccer player's activity. Then, the player's performance directly on the field will help the coaches understand which is the most important physiological component involved both in the technical movement and in all the biochemical changes occurring during the technical pause between two consecutive actions in a soccer match.

This book offers all the people working in soccer (fitness coaches, coaches, managers and players) all the basic information they need to further investigate training techniques and finally select the best ones in relation to the technical and biological outcome for every player in the context of his specific position and within his own group.

Therefore, I cannot but consider this work with the deepest interest, since it really aims at something real and fundamental, without falling into mere scientific semantics, which is definitely of critical importance.

Prof. Gianni Benzi MD, PhD
Institute of Pharmacology - Pavia University
Biochemical and Doping Committee - CONI Rome

Foreword

For more than twenty years I have been working in professional soccer circles. Since I have a particular bent for studying sport physiology, which means investigating how the human body works in the various disciplines - both because of my post-university career and my own interests and inclination - I have always tried to apply new ideas concerning athletic conditioning in soccer and I quickly exploited the first opportunity to do that in a Serie B Italian club. Every season I have endeavored to investigate this complex subject from the theoretical point of view, while also experiencing something new directly on the playing field.

Now, I would like to convey all my experiences and knowledge concerning the subject into this work, even though it is mainly confined to one single aspect: endurance. On other occasions (especially in the soccer magazine 'Il Nuovo Calcio') I have and will deal with other important themes. There are some who do not want to reveal their 'secrets', which means they do not want to say what they really know; on the contrary, I have always tried to communicate and let people know my personal experiences. Vincenzo Pincolini (fitness coach of Sacchi's A.C. Milan) often said that I invented the profession of the fitness coach; but, in reality, this is not true. When I started working in soccer, very few Italian clubs had their own fitness coaches; however, in the very rare cases where the fitness coach existed, his job was mainly confined to gym practice, while very little attention was focused on running and all the various kinds of running.

I immediately worked and struggled to introduce these important exercises in soccer, but also to help people understand the reason why specific training was key. In short, I tried to clearly explain what happens in the soccer player's muscles, circulation, organs and in the whole of his body while playing soccer, while also showing how it is possible - by means of constant training - to directly act on the body's structures and functions to improve the player's performance.

I am obviously very pleased that many Italian clubs at various levels have been following my training plans and suggestions. For instance: alternate one session of aerobic exercise (1 Km or similar distances repetitions) with one day of repeated sprints on hills during the pre-season training period; or combine aerobic exercise and practice to improve lactic acid capacity (even though this concerns a smaller number of teams) in the course of the soccer season.

I am even more delighted to see that my personal approach to the problem of athletic conditioning (starting from the analysis of how the body of the soccer player works and then acting on it, by means of regular training, in order to improve its efficiency) is now shared by nearly everybody in Italy. In my opinion, the difficulty in approaching some theoretical and practical aspects concerning physical conditioning in some countries stems mainly from the fact that the problem is not approached in this manner, which is complex at first, but helps to better reach the core of the question at a later stage.

I am also very pleased to hear that the figure of the fitness coach not only has been officially acknowledged by the Italian Soccer Association, but has also been included in the coaching staff of most clubs. I also tried to do my best to highlight the importance of this specialized figure in soccer to fellow coaches and experts as well as AIPAC, the Italian Association of Fitness Coaches in Soccer, which also played a crucial role in this context. I would like to encourage the executives of this association never to give up and always work for the cultural enrichment of its members. In my opinion, this is the best way to increase the number of soccer coaches who believe that the figure of the fitness coach is key and extremely beneficial to support their own jobs.

Some unjustified accusations

I shall admit that the role of the fitness coach and myself in particular have been attacked in different ways in the last few years - even though I believe these accusations are completely unjustified.

Among other things, I refer to one particular article by Enrico Lugo which appeared in the 'Notiziario del Settore Tecnico' - the magazine published by the Italian Soccer Association - (issue 7-8, July-August 1989). In that article I was referred to as the symbol of the introduction of what the author defines as 'scientific methodology of fitness training' in soccer. In practice, my scientific methods and I were accused of overlooking technical attributes, while also downplaying natural abilities and reducing the importance of soccer talent.

I immediately want to underline that I disagree for several reasons. First of all, I do not believe that today there are fewer top-class players than in the past. If we consider all the sports disciplines where the athlete's performance can be accurately 'measured' and analyzed (track and field, swimming, weight lifting, skating, track cycling...), we realize that the athletic performance is constantly progressing and that a number of athletes - sometimes very young - record times and measures which were almost unknown in the past. Moreover, some past filmed sequences concerning more subjective disciplines (gymnastics, diving...), clearly show that athletes were definitely less skillful than today. In short, performance levels in sports are constantly rising: and we should be amazed if this would not happen in soccer!

In the 1st October 1989 issue of the 'Gazzetta dello Sport' - the first Italian sports newspaper - Franco Arturi wrote that in the 60s there were many lower-class athletes playing in the Italian Serie A clubs and that most of those players could find no room at all in today's Serie C teams. According to Arturi, the improvement in the quality of the performance concerns defenders in particular. Most defending players in the past were characterized by 'rough feet', while today defenders have been considerably refining their technical skills.

To those who champion the soccer of the past, I would definitely suggest watching filmed sequences dating back to 30 or 40 years ago: whole matches, of course, and not selected fragments showing the best and most spectacular actions of the match. They would immediately realize that the play in the past was not so 'tight' as today. Players usually had plenty of time to control the ball, look around to assess the situation and then give the pass without any opponent approaching them. Today, the rhythm is much faster, the players without the ball move more, and those who receive the ball now have very little time to perform technical movements before the opponents attack them. Moreover, they need to develop some particular skills which most players did not have at all 30 or 40 years ago.

As to Lugo's assertion that better athletic efficiency (or the improvement in fitness training) necessarily obscures technical talent, I think it is completely wrong. In the same way as the painter needs to perfectly master the use of the brush and the sculptor the use of the chisel, those who use their bodies as a means to express their own talent - like soccer players - definitely benefit from improving their athletic efficiency. Top-class soccer players - some of the best stars of all time, like Gianni Rivera and Johan Cruyff - gradually began to cut poor figures when their physical efficiency started to worsen. However, the contrary is not true, which means that fitness training does not help to improve technical skills, but at least allows players to maintain the lucidity and the freshness to show their abilities throughout the 90 minutes of the match.

Even if there is a real drop from the technical point of view in modern soccer (though I agree with Arturi when he says there is no regression at all, but there is even an improvement at the technical level - while also considering that the rhythm of play is completely different today), what would fitness coaches' fault be in reality? Could Fleming be blamed because - since he invented penicillin, the first antibiotic drug, and therefore played a key role in reducing the number of deaths from infectious diseases - the number of deaths from cancer has grown considerably in the last few years?

In short, if by any chance modern soccer players had no specific technical skills (ball possession and so forth...), we could not blame fitness coaches but the coaches working in youth sectors who failed to adjust their players' technical development to the rhythms of modern soccer...

Moreover, somebody also accused me of spreading the idea that soccer players need to practice running more often. I refer you to another specific section of this book, the fourteenth chapter, where I will clearly reveal what I really think of this exercise - slow running - which is now considered as something worse than a poison for soccer players.

Acknowledgments

This book gives me the opportunity to do what I should have done long ago: that is the opportunity to thank all those who helped me in the world of soccer.

In the last twenty years or more, I got to know many players and coaches, some of whom became very popular, while others failed to achieve the success they had been longing for. I remember some of them with great pleasure and sympathy, also because they taught me many things.

Apart from Ferretto Ferretti (whose cooperation in writing this book was particularly precious) and other fitness coaches with whom I often came into contact for important and enriching discussions (in particular: Roberto Sassi, Vincenzo Pincolini, Fausto Anzil, Umberto Borino, Gigi Asnaghi, Massimo Begnis), I would like to thank all the coaches whom I worked with during my career, starting from the first, Pietro Maroso, and the person with whom I refined new coaching methods and who kindly allowed me to test many new ideas, Eugenio Fascetti. I also cultivated deep friendly relations with other coaches like Gian Piero Vitali, Vincenzo Guerini and Piero Frosio.

Furthermore, I would like to express my heartfelt thanks to Guido Borghi, the president of Varese Calcio, who asked me to work as the fitness coach of his club - playing in the Italian Serie B at that time - and Sandro Vitali, the manager of the club.

My special thanks to Italo Allodi, the person who invented the 'Supercorso' in Coverciano - the Italian course for professional soccer coaches organized by the National Soccer Association - and most contributed to the development of Italian soccer; Allodi actually called me to deliver a course of lectures on fitness training at the 'Supercorso', he kindly helped and supported me in several ways.

Those who should not read this book
I believe that reading this book would be completely useless for those who have the following ideas and do not intend to change their minds:
• in soccer nothing can be rationalized, and it is even useless to do

so since 'kicking the ball into the net' is the only thing which really counts;

- for training to be really effective it must repeat real-game situations and events; all the skills the player needs to play soccer can be practiced with the ball and athletic exercise without the ball (even if it is practiced for very short periods) is a mere waste of time;
- those who did not play soccer at professional levels cannot understand anything about soccer and can do nothing in the world of soccer.

In the course of the book I will try to explain the reason why, in my opinion, the first two beliefs are completely groundless. As to the third assertion, I would like you to remember that Arrigo Sacchi - coach of A.C. Milan, the Italian national team and now coach of Atletico Madrid - used to say that one does not need to have been a horse to become a jockey; while a theatre critic, who was often heavily attacked for not being qualified to judge plays since he wrote none, once answered that it is not necessary to be a hen to understand that the egg is rotten.

Enrico Arcelli

1

The Physical Attributes Required In Modern Soccer

In this book I especially focus my attention on how endurance should be trained in soccer players. However, this does not mean endurance is the only fundamental quality for them: on the contrary, I am absolutely convinced that they need to train many other physical attributes. That being said, I do believe that endurance, or better all the various components of endurance, must be of particular concern. Moreover, I want to underline that not only is it fundamental for the soccer player to train his aerobic endurance throughout the whole season, but I also think it is more useful and advisable to do it by practicing without the ball and according to specific criteria. Probably, it would be more pleasant for players (and also for the coaches who directly follow them) to practice by always using the ball; and it would also be convenient - as some believe - fitness training to be restricted to some jumps and sprints and nothing else. If many fitness coaches ask their players to endure strenuous physical exercise which obviously involves considerable workloads and fatigue levels (and they obviously know that the athletes won't be particularly happy when they are shown the training plan...), this means this is the best way for players to enhance their endurance levels.

In the last few years several factors have emerged which have further underlined the importance of the player's ability to run considerable distances during the course of a match, and which have therefore increased the need for higher levels of endurance. Among the main tactical reasons are: pushing the team up (compactness); movement without the ball; pressing and double teaming all over the field; prompt change of marking positions.

Is muscular explosiveness the sole important attribute for soccer players?

Those who are interested in soccer - even those who are simply fond of the sport - and have some acquaintance with motor activities could be convinced that for a person to be a skillful soccer player he must have '...well-developed lower limb muscles, particularly fit to generate great explosive power and able to make short and high-intensity efforts by using anaerobic energy mechanisms'.

However, these attributes are not enough: not only is it important for a soccer player to have powerful muscles allowing him to sprint or jump much better than average athletes but his body must also support him while repeating these and other movements over and over again during the course of the 90 minutes of a match.

Some years ago, an elite player who had just resumed playing after a serious injury asked me whether he could focus his training plan on sprint practice the following week, since he realized that his sprinting skills had proved very weak in the last thirty minutes of the match. At that point, I told him the story of the elderly woman who had an old pendulum clock which did not work; she decided to go to the clockmaker, but only took the pendulum to him, leaving the clock at home. The clockmaker asked why she only brought that piece, and the elderly woman promptly answered: "Because it is the pendulum which does not move any longer".

Many coaches tend to act like that old woman and therefore mistake consequences with causes. In short, if a soccer player can no longer sprint - especially in the final part of a match - they think he should practice as sprinters used to do in track and field, with long intervals between two consecutive sprints, so as to favor full recovery. But this is a great mistake: the week training cycle should obviously include sprinting practice with and without the ball, as well as those basic exercises (strength, rapidity, agility, explosive power and so forth) laying the necessary basis to improve - or at least constantly practice - one's sprinting skills. However, if maintaining fresh sprinting abilities throughout the whole match is the main purpose, it is also fundamental to constantly train all those components supporting repeated explosive power movements and all the other muscular movements occurring during the course of the match.

The most important physical attributes in soccer

Undoubtedly, there are several reasons for which some basic components of endurance (aerobic and lactic acid components, in particular) should be considered of critical importance in soccer - in addition to the qualities which we previously referred to at the beginning of the first paragraph and which, in short, could be defined as 'muscular explosiveness' attributes.

1.2.1 The importance of aerobic qualities

There is one particular value that physiologists have always considered a very significant indicator of the aerobic attributes of a person, his capability to produce ATP (the 'fuel' our muscles need for biological processes, see chapter four) by using oxygen. This value refers to maximal oxygen consumption, that is the maximum amount of oxygen our body can use per minute. In the sports disciplines where aerobic qualities are of critical importance - all the main long distance disciplines, like cross-country skiing, marathon or extended middle-distance racing, triathlon and so forth - topclass athletes usually have much higher values of maximal oxygen consumption than middle-level athletes, and their values often exceed 80 milliliters per kilogram of their body weight per minute (80 ml/Kg/min).

Soccer players cannot record such high values, because their physical characteristics are different from long-distance athletes' and because they also need to develop some other important physical attributes at the same time. However, the most recent data concerning high-level professional soccer players clearly show that maximal oxygen consumption values are higher on average in the last few years; for instance, Nowacki and his team in 1988 discovered an average of 69.2 ml/Kg/min in a German team.

Moreover, Reilly remembers that Smaros found out that maximal oxygen consumption has a very close connection not only with the total amount of kilometers the player covers during the course of a match, but also with the total number of sprints he makes in that period. Mognoni (1992) underlines the fact that in the Hungarian League some years ago the higher the average value of the players' maximal oxygen consumption, the better the position of the team in the final results (see diagram 1.1). The team winning the Hungarian League recorded an average value of 66.6 ml/Kg/min, those who were second, third and fifth in the final results had 64.3, 63.3 and 58.1 ml/Kg/min respectively.

The activity of mitochondrion enzymes is also an indicator of the capacity of muscles to use large amounts of oxygen per minute. According to Bengsbo and Mizuno the characteristics of the gastrocnemius (prominent muscle of the calf) mitochondrion enzymes of Danish soccer players were much more similar to long-distance athletes' than to those of athletes practicing strength disciplines.

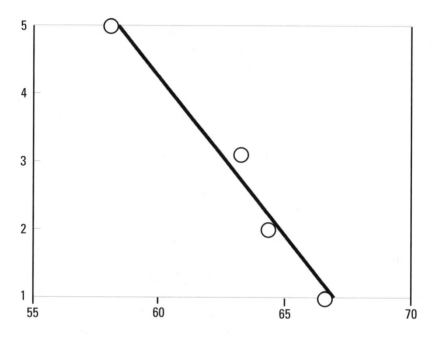

Diagram 1.1 - Final results of four teams playing in the first division Hungarian Soccer league in relation to their respective players' average maximal oxygen consumption. According to this research, the higher the value of maximal oxygen consumption, the better the team's final placing. From Mognoni (1992).

The importance of lactic acid components

As to the action of the lactic acid anaerobic mechanism, the data collected by the different authors tend to disagree with each other. However, the typical reference value is blood lactate concentration and this concentration is obviously influenced by several factors, starting from the performance of the single player and the general development of the match. In particular, if in the middle of the second half the score is already taken for granted or the players have no particular reason for going on fighting, lactate concentrations at the end of the match will undoubtedly be lower. The highest and somehow most interesting levels were discovered and analyzed by Ekblom (1986), who measured lactate concentrations of athletes playing in different divisions at the end of the first half and at the end of the whole match. He found out that (see diagram 8.2 in chapter eight) the higher the level of the team, the higher players' lactate concentrations on average. He also discovered that these values are higher after the first 45 minutes than at the end of the match, probably because muscle glycogen concentration gradually decreases as the end of the match approaches, as Karlsson had already highlighted in 1969 (see diagram 8.3 in chapter eight). In Ekblom's research average lactate concentrations in the blood of athletes playing in first division soccer leagues were more than 9 millimoles per liter after the first half and 7 millimoles per liter at the end of the whole match. On the contrary, lactate concentrations were nearly half of the above-mentioned values in the players belonging to the lowest division among those he considered for his research.

Classification of the main necessary attributes in soccer

When speaking of tennis - but the same can be said for soccer - Rossi (1990) states that the final result directly depends on an indefinite number of factors, abilities and skills, many of which can be regularly trained. He also adds that it is necessary to identify the most important ones in view of the final outcome - that is identify a hierarchy - so as not to waste time. Therefore, some components of endurance obviously appear to be of critical importance (according to what we have tried to explain up to now), it is however necessary to wonder whether they shall be mentioned with the most important attributes athletes need to play soccer and whether they should be given special attention while planning soccer players' conditioning.

According to Mognoni (1989), in order to identify the most typical attributes of high-level players it is first of all useful and advisable to measure these qualities by means of suitable tests carried out on several groups of athletes having different technical skills (for instance, players on the National team, the second and third divisions and also from amateur clubs) and then verify - through statistical confrontation - which are most relative to the particular level of the performance. In order to make things much simpler, let's imagine that the average values resulting from the tests designed for measuring one particular skill are very similar (or are not significantly different, if we want to be more accurate) in all the different groups of players. This clearly shows that this attribute is somehow of little importance. On the other hand, if the values decrease considerably when shifting from high to lower divisions, this obviously shows this quality is fundamental to become elite players.

Two years ago Mognoni studied all the information resulting from different tests collected by Roberto Sassi and concerning a number of teams playing in various divisions. The main differences resulted neither from strength tests (such as squat jump or counter-movement jump) nor from short-distance tests, but in all those exercises involving aerobic mechanisms, that is deflection speed in the Conconi-Sassi Test and the total distance covered by the athlete in the Cooper Test.

Mognoni believes that any method aimed at improving one's athletic performance must first be based on the accurate evaluation of the importance of each group of attributes, as well as of their capability to modify and adjust to the situation. Moreover, he also makes some remarks which would seem obvious at first, but which many coaches tend to forget. For instance, if it is proven that the performance depends by 0.5% on the width of a certain joint's range of motion, improving this particular feature does not really make sense, even though the athlete can easily work on it. Vice-versa, if standing height turned out to be particularly important, it would obviously be unhealthy to stretch the player to gain another half a centimeter.

Apart from the fact that a quality can be trained in specific ways or not, if we also consider the 'costs' in relation to the benefits it offers (when speaking of 'costs' I refer to all the conditioning hours this involves, the risks of injuries or other disorders, it's possible negative effects on other physical attributes, and so forth...), I am absolutely convinced that it is worthwhile focusing a particular part of soccer players' conditioning to all the various components of endurance. On the other hand, we already explained in the previous paragraphs that there are many different reasons for us to state that they are of critical importance in soccer and are strictly connected to the performance. Moreover, these qualities can certainly be modified by means of suitable training.

The importance of training endurance according to rational criteria

As a dietitian I obviously have a wide knowledge on many different slimming diets; however, some particular magazines often advertise completely new diets which are a bit strange. Many of them can actually help people to slim down (or, better, to lose weight), because they provide the body with a lower amount of calories than the total quantity it needs to counterbalance daily calorie loss. However, only a very few of them really help people to slim down in a healthy way, which means they stimulate a decrease in body fat concentration without impairing neither physical efficiency nor muscle mass and without causing any deficiency in some of the most important nutrients.

I would say that the same can be said for endurance training in soccer. There are still some people who believe that any exercise involving hard effort and causing fatigue is sufficient to improve the peculiar endurance skills of soccer players. There are some coaches who think they have been working perfectly during the pre-season training period because their training plan included long walking in the woods, or because it was based on several series of 1000 meter running repetitions, without dividing the players into different groups and suggesting a specific pace for each group, but setting the same final time every player. Other coaches, on the contrary, ask their players to run just once covering a 300-meter distance with the greatest effort possible. And they are all satisfied and convinced that they have worked properly since their players are fatigued. Some years ago some even thought that if a player had no painful lower limb muscles at the beginning of the pre-season training period, this necessarily meant he hadn't been working properly!

It is proven that in many cases - as will be explained in chapter eleven dealing with the mental components of endurance - there is no improvement if there is no fatigue, however the contrary is not true: this means that fatigue and high-intensity effort do not necessarily have a positive effect on the athlete's body. In reality, in order to improve each one of the components of endurance necessary in soccer, the most effective stimulus must have extremely specific characteristics. If these elements are not taken into proper account, training will be increasingly useless. Since training periods are always very short in soccer - especially the time dedicated to conditioning - it is absolutely unreasonable to waste time by practicing useless exercises of little or no importance at all in view of the final goal.

The importance of practicing without the ball

When referring to fitness training of any sports discipline, one could wonder whether it is absolutely necessary for an athlete to do something different from what that particular sport directly involves in order to train his body to make the best performance possible. In other words, when referring to soccer isn't it enough for the athlete to play soccer exclusively to develop the best efficiency in view of the soccer match? In the same way, can't the tennis player properly practice by simply playing tennis and nothing else?

'Imitating the match', referring to the peculiar features of the match and trying to simulate them, is undoubtedly the simplest, the oldest and the most elementary way for a coach to select training methods. In practice, this implies nothing else but reproducing and repeating the match or part of it: the high jumper will endeavor to clear the bar at the highest point possible; the discus thrower will try to throw the discus as far as possible; the 800-meter runner will practice by covering similar distances - 600 meters, for instance - at a very close pace to that of the official race; soccer players (as well as field hockey or rugby players) will train by playing matches approaching real game situations, though they could modify some basic rules concerning the number of players, the size of the field or the duration of the game.

Certainly, there are some prerequisite aspects in this conditioning method, at least because the athletes are faced with some particular problems (physical, psychological, technical, tactical and so forth...) they must also handle during the match. This is why any soccer or basketball coach would never ask his athletes to face very important matches without including some specific training games in the conditioning period immediately preceding the match.

Nevertheless, if a coach really wants to train his players in the best way possible, simply imitating the match cannot be the most effective method, because there are some particular physical attributes which cannot be properly trained. Let's look at a quality like jumping. Training games and friendly matches cannot help the defender who is particularly lacking in this attribute to definitely improve it. Generally speaking, the simple imitation of the match is very unlikely to perfectly combine all the different 'training stimuli' with the most suitable qualitative and quantitative characteristics aimed at developing those physical changes and improvements which could occur by means of specific training methods.

In soccer, for instance, it is definitely very difficult - and I think it is even impossible - to train some components of endurance in a really effective manner by practicing with the ball. In particular:
using the ball makes it extremely difficult for the player to practice for some minutes or a number of seconds by maintaining his phys-

ical effort near the anaerobic threshold (or better, slightly above it), which is the most specific stimulus for the definite improvement of peripheral aerobic components.

In order to improve those components of lactic acid capacity which are of critical importance for soccer players, it is advisable to reach such lactate concentrations which make it very difficult for the athlete to properly perform technical movements with the ball.

Coaches sometimes try to plan and coach some exercises involving the use of the ball while also aiming at training specific physical attributes at the same time. However, not only can this kind of practice not achieve this final goal, it can neither help the player's technical improvement in most cases. In short, such a training method is nearly useless.

Why should players practice with the ball during the whole training session as some people firmly believe? Can this kind of aprioristic choice be considered something really rational in a pragmatic background like the world of sport? Are you really sure that professional and amateur teams cannot devote part of their training sessions (it is a matter of minutes, of course!) to specific conditioning exercises aimed at effectively improving all those components of endurance which soccer players really need? And why do those who believe that conditioning practice without the ball tires players out at the psychological level not think that if the players get tired when practicing without the ball, they can also feel weary while working too much with the ball?

Endurance

W hat does the word 'endurance' refer to in sport? An expert in sports disciplines could find it very simple to give a definition of this physical attribute. He could easily understand why an athlete is more capable of physical endurance than another or when endurance is key to stand out in a particular discipline. But the reality is a bit more complex than one would imagine, especially because endurance has several physical components (and psychological, too). Moreover, depending on the particular sports discipline one refers to, the single most important components can vary as well as their global significance in relation to the final goals of the physical performance in that discipline.

The most important definitions of "endurance"

If one wants to realize the complexity of this physical attribute which is commonly defined as endurance, he or she can simply consider all the various definitions given by some important experts studying all the different aspects of sport. Here are some of the main definitions (some other explanations appear in the table 2.1, from Sotgiu, 1988):

Harre (1972): "When referring to any sports activity, endurance defines the ability of the body to endure fatigue while practicing for extended periods of time".

Morehouse and Miller (1978): "Endurance can be considered as the ability of the body to bear all the stresses deriving from prolonged physical exercise".

Ulatowski (1979): "Endurance is the capability of the body to suffer physical effort over extended periods of time; it is the ability to overcome resistance, perform prolonged exercise and locomotor movements of long duration".

Table 2.1
Here are some other interpretations of the word 'endurance' given by some important sport scientists; these definitions are included in the book 'Coordination Skills and Endurance' by Paolo Sotgiu.

Filin: 'Endurance is the ability of the body or of the human being as a whole to resist and oppose fatigue'.

Carabelli: 'Endurance is the physical attribute allowing the individual to withstand physical effort over an extended period of time, during which the body opposes the rising symptoms of fatigue by applying to all the possible sources of muscular and psychological energy'.

Manno: 'Endurance - physical attribute of the human being - can be defined as the capability to endure fatigue in long-duration exercise'.

Nabatnikowa: 'The word endurance usually means the ability of the individual to prolong physical exercise over a period of time. However, in order to clarify the question it is also advisable to consider the concept of 'performance capacity', which is much wider and more comprehensive, since it defines the capability to perform high-intensity exercise in relation to the duration of the performance itself'.

Zaciorskj (1970): "Endurance means the ability to perform any physical activity for extended periods of time, without this lowering its real effective nature; in other words, endurance can be defined as the capacity to withstand fatigue".

Tschiene (cited by Scarselli, 1989): "General endurance is the capability of the athlete to endure, over an extended period of time, any physical workload involving several muscle groups and being in positive connection with a particular sports discipline".

Peronnet (cited by Scarselli, 1989): "Endurance can be defined as the ability of a person to use a large percentage of his/her maximal oxygen consumption for extended periods of time".

Scarselli (1989): "Endurance is a physical attribute which can be trained and improved; it is characterized by prolonged exercise, no matter how it is performed, generated by the harmonious combination of several mechanisms - metabolic, organic and psychological - in relation to the athletic bio-individuality of the subject".

You can immediately realize that the definitions given by the various experts do not perfectly agree with each other. Harre's definition, for instance, highlights two very important aspects of endurance: the fatigue threshold and the long duration of physical exercise. In the two following explanations - given by Morehouse and Miller and by Ulatowski respectively - the attention is mainly focused on the changes occurring in the body while practicing prolonged physical exercise and which the body must properly resist; moreover, they also seem to include implicit reference to the psychological factors of endurance. The definition given by Zaciorskij lays particular emphasis on the fact that endurance allows the athlete to maintain his/her efficiency at constant levels during the whole performance. While the previous interpretations implied that a decrease in the body's efficiency is very likely to occur when practicing aerobic exercise as the body gradually approaches fatigue threshold (the more the body can resist fatigue, the smaller the decrease in the body's efficiency). Zaciorskij's definition especially concentrates on the importance of avoiding any drop in the body's efficiency level. This is particularly interesting when compared to the specific nature of endurance in soccer players. Tschiene's interpretation introduces some new elements and special reference is made to the importance of the muscle mass involved in the physical exercise.

The definition given by Peronnet has a purely physiological basis and seems to be more fit for typically aerobic constant-intensity sports disciplines such as the marathon and cross-country skiing than for sports games. Finally, Scarselli underlines that there are many and various elements which influence the athlete's ability to handle endurance performances.

A more detailed definition

Since the main sport experts have considerably different opinions as to the accurate interpretation of the word 'endurance' - which clearly shows how difficult it is to find a comprehensive but simple and short definition - on the occasion of the first International Congress of Sport Medicine applied to Soccer in 1979, Sassi and I worked out the following detailed definition which could include and highlight all the various aspects of endurance in the different sports disciplines:

Endurance is an athletic quality directly influencing the performance of the athletes of many sports: it is fundamental in some disciplines (in middle and long-distance racing in track and field; in several swimming and cycling races; in cross-country skiing and so forth); and it is an important but not a key factor in other sports (some team games, for instance, soccer, basketball, field hockey and so on).

In the disciplines where this attribute plays a role of crucial importance, endurance can mean the ability to generate the maximum amount of work in relation to:

- *the time of the performance: it can vary from a number of seconds to several minutes and more;*
- *muscle groups involved: depending on the sport, they can account for a very small percentage (very few muscle groups), or*
- *a considerable percentage of the whole body mass.*

In those disciplines where endurance is an important but not a prerequisite element, the definition could mainly focus on the fact that the athlete can still perform technical movements in the most proper and accurate manner despite his muscles having already endured prolonged aerobic exercise.

In those disciplines where this physical attribute plays a crucial role, endurance can also be considered as the result of several body functions combined together, which can be more or less important according to the time of the performance and the muscle groups involved in that particular physical activity.

However, it is practically impossible to offer a biological and technical definition of endurance which could fit all the various sports disciplines.

Endurance is influenced by two main groups of factors: the mechanisms by which energy is used by the body and the processes providing the body with the energy it needs.

As far as energy consumption is concerned, the performance of the athlete capable of physical endurance depends on the mechanical performance in part -- which results from several technical, stylistic, physical factors -- and partly on various anatomical and functional characteristics such as muscular elasticity. Moreover, both psychological and motivational factors also play a crucial role.

As to energy availability (that is providing the muscles with the suitable amount of energy they need to work effectively), it is possible to state that it is mainly influenced by aerobic and lactic acid anaerobic energy mechanisms, whose importance (in percentage) varies especially in relation to the duration of the performance.

When referring to soccer in particular, endurance could be defined as: The ability to maintain the performance at constant levels for as long as possible (from the physical, technical and tactical ... points of view) despite the body having already worked considerably.

The Laws of Training

Until a few years ago people thought that the training methods used in one particular sport could not be applied to another sports discipline. In particular, soccer was considered as a separate world, with no possible connection with other sports - especially by those who were directly involved in that world. In reality, on one side it is perfectly true that every sport has its own peculiar features, but on the other hand, it is also true that various training methods produce highly specific changes in the athlete's body and that there are some 'laws' regulating such important changes. The 'theory of training' -- which was mainly developed by Soviet scientists -- especially concentrates on these basic laws. For years I have been working to suggest an alternative solution to the theory of training, that is focusing the attention on how the body really works, on the 'physiological models' of one particular sports discipline and all the changes which are likely to occur in the body because of constant training.

From Soviet training methods to physiological models

In 1965 I was working at the Institute of Human Physiology at Milan University and was especially concerned with the mechanics of running and muscular elasticity; and at that very time the first works in the world concerning elastic recovery in running were published. At the same time, Prof. Margaria's worldwide renown was also due to his personal research on muscular energetics, which means how muscle tissue produces the energy it needs to work. I was obviously interested in that subject and kept constantly up to date and, since I was also a young track and field coach, I endeavored to spread these concepts in the world of track and field -- which was something absolutely new -- by using a very simple language which coaches could easily understand, while also trying to combine these new ideas with what the coaches could directly observe in their athletes. I wrote a long article where I tried to explain some basic physiological concepts. For instance, I explained that muscle tissue uses a particular 'fuel' called ATP to produce energy and therefore work; that 100 meter racing is strictly connected with non-lactic acid mechanisms, marathon racing with the aerobic mechanism, while 400 meter and fast middle distance racing also involve lactic acid processes, which are characterized by the production of lactic acid; and so forth. I also tried to help people to understand that those physiological elements were strictly connected not only with the final outcome in the performance, but also with everyday choices the coach has to make when planning his athletes' training. In most cases, the reasons why one particular kind of exercise is better than another can actually be understood only if one perfectly knows some specific physiological concepts.

Somebody in the world of track and field clearly told me that my article had caused great confusion in the minds of most coaches and that, in short, my publication had brought nothing but damage. However, a few months later some track and field coaches -- the youngest, in particular -- were already using some words such as 'aerobic power' or 'lactic acid capacity' very correctly, and when they planned their training sessions, they often explained their goals from the physiological point of view. At least, that article was useful to finally connect two separate worlds (the world of research and that of sport) which had been completely separate until then and had no possibility to communicate since the languages they had been speaking were so different.

When I began to work in the world of soccer as official doctor with the youth team of Varese Soccer Club four years later, I immediately realized that soccer coaches and experts did not know those concepts at all. Some time before, the general manager of the Italian sports newspaper 'La Gazzetta dello Sport' had encouraged me to write and publish some articles concerning soccer players' conditioning. My ideas would sound obvious today, but most people thought they could not be applied to soccer at that time. In general, I was always told that 'Soccer is something different' - a refrain which I heard plenty of times from that moment on. Those who were used to repeating that phrase were absolutely convinced that soccer coaching could not apply some basic concepts of critical importance in other sports. It was very difficult for me to accept that remark; my great mistake was to believe that it was quite simple to understand that, once the individual clearly realizes how the body works when performing various physical efforts (during a cycling or swimming race, for instance, as well as in the course of a soccer match), it is much easier for him or her to use suitable training methods aimed at stimulating such physical changes so as to help the body to make a better physical performance. In soccer, very few people were willing to 'plunge into the human body' and this was absolutely essential for them to finally understand how the athlete's complex machine really works.

My career as fitness coach in soccer

Later I got another job in the world of soccer and began to work as a fitness coach almost by chance. Pietro ('Peo') Maroso was the coach of Varese Calcio Under 18 team and, since I was the official doctor assigned to that group and therefore followed them during their home matches and training sessions, I could immediately suggest to the coach the best solutions and the suitable training methods he could apply each time we realized that one particular player had specific problems and deficiencies (when he was weak in sprint running or was capable of little endurance, for instance). Probably I was so persistent that, when a heavy snowfall made playing fields completely unplayable Maroso asked me if I felt up to planning and supervising his players' fitness training for a certain period I accepted with great pleasure and -- according to soccer experts' opinions - the results were very positive.

In that period, the first team of Varese Calcio Club was playing in the Italian Serie A League. In the 1971-72 soccer season the team was not very lucky: at the early stages of the season Varese Calcio was at the bottom of the league and finished with only 13 points. Before the end of that season relegation was definitely obvious. The president of the club -- Guido Borghi (who was very young and open-minded) -- asked me if I was willing to become the fitness coach of the first team in the Serie B the following year. My only condition (which aroused some perplexity at the beginning, but was finally accepted) was that I could work with the players for about 10 days before they left on holiday. I wanted to know the athletes I was going to train the following season and I also wanted them to get used to some particular training methods. I also asked the club to hire my brother-in-law, Massimo Begnis, who had been a member of the Italian track and field team several times, held the Italian record in the 3 Km hurdle racing and was a professor of physical training at that time. Maroso was promoted to coach of the first team; 14 players who had played in the Serie A League the previous season were finally sold and no other new element arrived, apart from those who had been playing on loan in lower division clubs and whom I already knew, since they had played in the Under 18 team. Many people immediately predicted that the team would be relegated to the Serie C League.

Against all the negative expectations, the team performed very well during the course of that season which marked the beginning of my long career as fitness coach. The team finished in fifth place and the players showed an incredible athletic efficiency during the whole season: most people actually wondered at our players' speed and endurance, in particular. No other teams were basing their conditioning plans on specific running exercises at that time.

Many asked what kind of training I suggested to the players of Varese Calcio to make them so efficient, and I always tried to explain the basic reasons underlying my final choices. But most people seemed not to be interested in what I was saying: nobody wanted to 'get into the machine', nobody wanted to know how it really works: they only wanted to see the final training tables and plans.

The modern soccer player

In 1973, I wrote 'The Modern Soccer Player'. I expressly wrote that work to help people realize how important it is to perfectly understand how the 'human machine' works in all its components and as a whole. The book dealt with muscular and cardiovascular adaptation and improvement, training methods with specific attention focused on their effects on the human body and so forth. Those concepts were absolutely new in the world of soccer and I obviously aroused various reactions, many of them negative. A very popular coach asked me if the book included all the possible gym exercises for all the different muscles of the body when he knew that my work was focused on athletic conditioning. Then, when I answered that there was none he was definitely surprised and told me he could not understand how I could write a complete book on fitness training. Some other famous coaches were convinced that my ideas could not be applied to soccer players.

That book is obviously outdated today. In the last few years I have been realizing that new ideas evolve very rapidly, specifically as far as training methods are concerned. The basic concepts of soccer had crystallized for many years, but they gradually began to improve and evolve very quickly starting from that moment on. However, I think that nobody can deny that I definitely opened a new path. Those who are too young to know how things really went can easily understand the importance of those changes by looking at how fitness training was referred to before that period.

The importance of looking into the 'box'

When I was working in track and field, I was specifically concerned with middle and long distance racing. In 1977, I clearly spoke of a 'theoretical model', by referring it to marathon racing. Then, the following year I specifically focused my attention on the 'theoretical model' of the soccer player and on the best way to implement it in order to rationalize athletic conditioning.

What does 'theoretical model' mean? How can the 'theoretical model' be connected to training methods?

At this point, I must take a step backward to answer these questions. For some years, I had been teaching 'Theory of training' - the subject studying the laws which regulate the changes occurring in the athlete's body as a result of physical conditioning -- at the College of Physical Training in Milan. Frequently, some of the students attending my course came to me and told me that I was not teaching the 'real' theory of training according to them. They had read either the works published by some popular Soviet authors, who had first studied that subject, or those written by their Italian 'disciples' and realized that I was explaining those concepts in a different manner.

As I highlighted in an article which appeared in the magazine 'Sport and Medicine', the standard theory of training developed by Soviet authors is typically 'behavioral'. Behaviorists were those psychologists who studied all those manifestations which could be observed in animals, children and adults such as ordinary behaviors, learning processes and the possible reactions to one stimulus and whose leader was John B. Watson (1878-1958). Unlike all the psychologists preceding and following them, they expressly concentrated on the behavior and did not try to investigate the mind, that is how the brain works. In short, from their point of view the brain could be defined as a "closed box".

The standard theory of training has very similar features: in practice, it does not focus the attention on what happens in the human body as a result of physical training. If we want to use an I.T. metaphor, the classic theory of training only deals with the input and the output, that is the conditioning methods (which means training plans and tables, in practice) and the changes in the athlete's performance (which means how the results of specific tests which the athlete is regularly subjected to gradually change). On the contrary, it completely neglects what happens in the body as a result of athletic conditioning, that is all the specific changes occurring in the athlete's body when he regularly practices a certain kind of physical exercise. From such a point of view, those who support and analyze this theory of training therefore consider the body as a "closed box" (diagram 3.1).

This approach somehow prevents them from clearly understanding some of the basic aspects of training in sport. On one hand I think that the standard Soviet approach to athletic conditioning has played a role of considerable importance, on the other side I also believe that it is absolutely necessary to get rid of all the bonds of the "behavioral doctrine". Moreover, I am convinced that for us to understand how the body works and adapts to the various conditioning methods we could derive considerable help from the increasingly flourishing scientific research applied to sport and focusing, in the last few years in particular, on what I would define as "no man's land", the reality of combining physiology and training which was hardly investigated in the past.

The theory of training on a physiological basis

It is useful and advisable to open the "closed box" and look inside it. In this way, it is also possible to better understand what coaching really means. Therefore, the diagram representing the standard theory of training - that of the so called "closed box", (see diagram 3.1) - should be replaced by the diagram 3.2. Training stimulates the athlete's body to gradually adapt to the new condition and this adaptation process finally results in a significant improvement in the athlete's performance.

However, the main changes in the athlete's performances (which means in the results of the tests he is subjected to) can develop for several reasons. It is therefore important to identify which one really prevails over the others and for this to be possible, it is necessary to know and understand all the inner mechanisms which directly influence the performance.

For instance, strength can improve either because of a physical change in the muscle tissue, or because the orders directly deriving from the brain have changed. In the same way, the aerobic components of endurance can improve because of either central or periph-

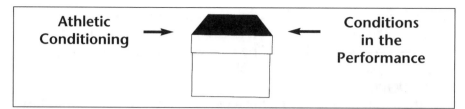

Diagram 3.1 - The standard theory of training does not deal with all the adaptation processes occurring in the athlete's body as a result of athletic conditioning, but only focuses the attention on input (= athletic conditioning) and output (= changes in the athlete's performances).

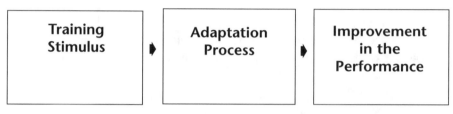

Diagram 3.2 - It is advisable to replace the standard theory of training diagram (diagram 3.1) with this new model where athletic conditioning (or better, 'the training stimulus') causes an important adaptation process in the athlete's body, which finally results in an improvement in the performance.

eral adaptation processes, and so forth. The basic conditioning tests should also change their functions in relation to the new model: not only should they be used to assess and control the changes in the athleteís performances, but they should also help to understand what happens inside the body.

The coach and the 'inner consistency' method

Some fellow researchers agree that coaches and fitness trainers do not coach in a 'scientific' manner, in the sense that there is no scientific evidence of the real effectiveness of most training tools and methods. In general, I reply that training methods evolve so quickly in sports -- specifically in such disciplines as track and field -- that those who wait for the irrefutable evidence of the effectiveness of the methods they are using would inevitably be defeated by those who do not attend to such confirmation, but trust their powers of observation and intuitions exclusively.

I would like to add another concept which I am particularly concerned with: even when the research offers no specific proof that a certain kind of physical exercise is the most effective for the final improvement of one particular physical attribute, one can however choose that kind of work. In this case, the choice is based on an inductive process which could be defined as 'inner consistency' principle. If a coach coherently combines together - like a detective or a person doing a jigsaw puzzle - the data (many or few) he can obtain at a theoretical level, those which can be deduced logically and the information he can collect by regularly observing the changes resulting from a particular kind of athletic conditioning, his choices are not 'scientific' but can be considered absolutely rational.

It is evident that one cannot grow so fond of the choices he has made that he believes they are the only possible solutions. On the contrary: every coach should be mentally ready to rethink all his ideas in case he gets new information evidence which is in conflict with what he has been planning up to that moment.

The power of observation of the coach plays a role of critical importance. Some coaches are convinced that they will be held in higher esteem if they act as 'scientists', that is if they speak of mitochondrions or type II muscle fibers and so forth. On the contrary, I usually hold them in greater esteem when they successfully combine suitable theoretical knowledge and considerable power of observation, i.e. when they are able to observe their athletes, their reactions to a particular kind of exercise, the short and long-term effects of a certain training method and so on.

From the theoretical model to the training plans

The next chapters will deal with the 'theoretical model' of the soccer player's physiological attributes. In short, I will try to describe how the muscles, the heart and all the other organs and tissues of the soccer player work during the course of a match. I would like to underline the main stages for a coach to rationally plan the most suitable training methods which best suit the soccer player:

1 - set a theoretical model of the soccer player specifically
focusing attention on how his body really works ('physiological model');

2 - from that model start to assess how and where the athlete's body should change and improve;

3 - regularly compare the theoretical data with what is taking place and the characteristics of the theoretical model with that of a single player or the team, in particular;

4 - draw up a conditioning program while also taking into account several important factors: the main goals to achieve,

specific deadlines to achieve those goals, the time one has at his disposal and so forth.

An outline of the soccer player's physiological model

How is it possible to describe how the body of a soccer player works while he is playing a soccer match? In other words, what is the 'physiological model' of the soccer player?

By simplifying what is taking place, you will find that the intensity of the soccer player's physical effort varies considerably during the course of a match: in some moments it can be very low (when the player is standing motionless or is moving sideways, for instance); in other cases, it can even account for a large number of calories per minute (when he sprints or jumps to head the ball, for example).

There are some particular moments in the match when the soccer player's energy requirements are three times higher than usual (when he sprints very rapidly, for instance). In other cases, his energy requirements can be as much as five times lower than the average (when he is walking, for instance) (see table 3.1).

Our muscles always use a particular kind of 'fuel' - ATP - to work, and this substance can have different origins as will be explained in chapter four. If we consider every single movement the soccer player can make during a match (a sprint, a jump, tackle, jog, run backwards), we should speak of 'non lactic acid' ATP, which means that ATP is already stored in muscles or is derived from CP (creatine phosphate). Moreover, if we consider that the soccer player's physical work is somehow constant - as far as this can be referred to such a discipline as soccer - we should remember that, apart from the oxygen linked to myoglobin and already stored in muscle fibers, the muscle tissue also gets a certain amount of oxygen from the blood every minute, and this oxygen is expressly used to 'produce' aerobic ATP. Aerobic ATP satisfies only part - and it is sometimes a very small part - of the total energy requirement, specifically in case of high-intensity physical exercise. It accounts for about 10% in a quick sprint for instance and for up to 35% in a burst of speed (this could be the kind of movement the outside back makes to recover into his defensive line from the opposing area). On the contrary, aerobic ATP can completely satisfy all the energy requirements of a player walking (see table 3.1).

After the first sprint or burst of speed of the match, the player is already in a condition of non lactic acid oxygen deficit. A very short period (we speak of seconds) of very low intensity exercise or absolute rest would suffice to make up the deficit completely. However, if we remember that the soccer player makes 3.5 to 6 running movements per minute on average -- 1.5 to 2.5 of which are usually sprints or bursts of speed -- we realize that he cannot always compensate for his non lactic acid oxygen debt. Furthermore, the various phases of the game can even force the player to get involved in a new physical effort (in order to follow his direct opponent or

Kind of Effort	Energy Requirements	Non Lactic Acid ATP
Sudden sprint (10 meters starting from a standing position in 2 seconds)	900 cal/Kg/min	750 to 840 cal/Kg/min
Spurting movement at a speed of 20 mph.	520 cal/Kg/min	370 to 460 cal/Kg/min
Spurting movement at a speed of 15 mph.	320 cal/Kg/min	170 to 260 cal/Kg/min
Running movement at a speed of 8 mph.	150 cal/Kg/min	0 to 90 cal/Kg/min
Walking movement at a speed of 4.5 mph	100 cal/Kg/min	0 to 40 cal/Kg/min
Walking movement at a speed of 3 mph	60 cal/Kg/min	

Table 3.1
This table shows the energy requirements (second column) - expressed in calories per every kilogram of body weight per minute - for some of the various kinds of efforts the soccer player can make during the course of a match. Moreover, it also includes (third column) the approximate values of ATP produced through the non lactic acid mechanism. In practice, this refers to the non lactic acid oxygen deficit the soccer player is very likely to accumulate by performing these kinds of physical movements.

take his starting position, for instance) before his oxygen deficit has been fully made up. In this way, the oxygen debt increases constantly. This is why the muscles of the soccer player produce ATP through the so-called lactic acid mechanism, that is the mechanism by which lactic acid is finally manufactured. (For further details see chapter four).

The Energy Components
of Endurance

The word 'energetics' often frightens sport coaches and experts in general. This term simply refers to all the mechanisms by which muscles produce the energy they need to work. In this context, it is first of all necessary to explain some important concepts:

- muscles use the biochemical energy stored in one particular molecule: the ATP molecule;
- muscles can be considered engines, since they can exploit the biochemical energy of ATP to generate motion;
  therefore, ATP is the 'fuel' of muscles, the only source of energy they can use;
- while we fill our cars up with a foreign substance (gasoline) muscles need to manufacture ATP by themselves; the higher the intensity of muscle effort, the larger the amount of ATP they need to produce per second;
- most ATP is produced during physical effort by using the energy deriving from other molecules - from sugars and fats of food, in particular.

A high-level soccer player usually spends 17.4 kilocalories per minute on average which correspond to the total amount of calories a runner needs to maintain a constant speed of about 10 mph and, therefore, to cover a distance of about 18 miles at a uniform pace in the 90 minutes corresponding to a whole soccer match. On the contrary, the soccer player usually sprints, stops, restarts, changes his direction or completely turns about, runs backward or sideways and so forth. This means that he covers a shorter distance during the course of the whole competition. However, this causes the player to spend many kilograms of ATP in every soccer match!

ATP production

ATP is the English acronym for adenosine triphosphate. The ATP molecule consists of four elementary molecules, one adenosine (adenine linked to D-ribose) and three phosphate groups, linearly linked together by covalent bonds; the molecule can be schematically depicted as follows:

adenosine ------P--*--P--*--P

As you can see, each phosphate molecule is represented by the letter P. However, while the phosphate nearest to the adenosine molecule is linked with a simple dash, the two other phosphate groups are linked together with a different symbol (--*--); these are two specific bonds which are usually defined as 'high energy bonds', since they generate great amounts of energy when they break down, and this energy is fully exploited by muscles to work. The reaction by which ATP releases energy can be schematically represented as follows:

adenosine-----P--*--P--*--P = adenosine-----P--*--P + P+ + energy

The molecule resulting from this chemical reaction consists of adenosine and two phosphate groups (one phosphate has a high energy bond, while the other has a normal bond) and is known as ADP, or adenosine diphosphate.

Since a very small amount of ATP is stored in muscles and this amount is sufficient to endure very short physical exercise, muscles must constantly produce ATP by themselves. Muscle tissue can manufacture new 'fuel' starting from what was left after the previous ATP molecules had released their energy, that is starting from ADP and the phosphate group (P). The production of fresh ATP occurs because of very complex enzyme systems in muscles, which allow them to get energy from other molecules. As was explained before, these important molecules usually derive from food.

Remember that fresh ATP can be produced in different ways, three in particular which are outlined below. The better one can understand how these mechanisms work and can be enhanced, the more rational athletic conditioning in soccer will be.

Apart from the minimum amount of ATP already stored in muscles at the beginning of the match, the remaining ATP (several kilograms, as was said before) is manufactured during the match in one of these ways, that is through one of the following 'energy mechanisms':

- the non lactic acid anaerobic energy mechanism, where oxygen is not involved and no lactic acid is produced; in this case, the energy necessary to produce ATP is released by one particular molecule - phosphocreatine (CP) - which also consists of a high energy bond;
- the lactic acid anaerobic energy mechanism, where oxygen is not involved, but lactic acid is manufactured in muscles; the energy necessary to synthesize ATP is provided by sugar molecules which are gradually broken down to form lactic acid;
- the aerobic energy mechanism, taking place with the presence of oxygen in muscles; energy is normally provided by the combination of oxygen with sugar (combustion of glucose with oxygen, carefully regulated by specific enzymes) or fats and a very small amount of proteins.

In all the above mentioned energy mechanisms, one phosphate molecule (P) binds to one ADP molecule by means of a high energy bond. In this way, a second high energy bond generates and a new ATP molecule is produced. For this second bond to form, a suitable amount of energy must be provided. However, in each of the three mechanisms energy is provided in a different way. In the following paragraphs you will find some useful information - the most important features from the practical point of view, at least - about the three energy mechanisms of muscles.

The non lactic acid anaerobic mechanism

It typically concerns physical exercise lasting a very short time. If a soccer player starts from a phase of total rest, sprints a few meters, jumps, or kicks the ball, his muscles use up the ATP provided by phosphocreatine in addition to that already stored in muscle tissue. Phosphocreatine consists of a creatine molecule combined with a phosphate group. These two elementary molecules are linked together by means of a high energy bond (--*--) as follows:

creatine--*--P

When the --*-- bond breaks down, a certain amount of energy is released, which is used to produce ATP starting from ADP and phosphate (P).

This energy mechanism is defined as 'anaerobic' because it does not require oxygen. Furthermore, it is a 'non lactic acid' process since it does not bring about lactate production. However, the total quantity of ATP provided by this mechanism is quite small, since CP stores in muscles are very low. Although CP stores can never be used completely (nearly half of them can be exploited), they allow the synthesis of a total amount of ATP which is nearly four times larger than the quantity stored in muscle tissue at the beginning of physical effort. The advantage is that the non lactic acid anaerobic mechanism manufactures a much larger amount of ATP (which can therefore be used by muscles) per second than the lactic acid mechanism (nearly twice) and the aerobic one (nearly threefold). In other words, the phosphocreatine mechanism is definitely more powerful than the others.

The lactic acid anaerobic mechanism

It is also known as 'anaerobic glycolysis process', since sugar molecules are broken down ('glycolysis') in a series of biochemical reactions not involving oxygen ('anaerobiosis'). Sugar molecules (for a more accurate explanation: glucose molecules) are not broken down completely until lactic acid is finally produced. In reality, as it will be clearly explained in chapter eight, one lactate ion (LA-) and one hydrogen ion (H+) form in muscles in addition to the energy needed to synthesize ATP from ADP and phosphate (P):

$$glucose = LA^- + H^+ + energy$$

Both lactate and the hydrogen ion are 'waste products' which are very likely to cause serious disorders to muscle tissue (for further details see chapter eight). They can leave muscle fibers during the course of a match and enter the blood stream; and during the 90 minutes of a soccer match, they can be excreted by the blood.

In general, a well-trained soccer player playing a low-intensity match is supposed to produce very small amounts of lactic acid. During a high intensity match, on the contrary, where players are required to sprint frequently with short rests, large amounts of lactate store up in the athlete's muscles and continuously flow into the blood stream. Therefore lactate concentration inevitably grows beyond standard levels, although the mechanisms responsible for removing it are promptly activated.

The aerobic mechanism

In this case (like in the lactic acid anaerobic mechanism) the energy exploited to synthesize ATP can also be provided by glucose molecules. But, unlike the above-mentioned process, glucose molecules are completely broken down to carbon dioxide and water through a long chain of biochemical reactions. Apart from glucose, energy can also be produced starting from fats, or, for a more accurate description, from free fatty acids, which are also completely oxidized to carbon dioxide and water. The biochemical reactions leading to energy production can be schematically represented as follows:

Like in the two other energy mechanisms, the term 'energy' refers to the energy that muscle tissue needs to synthesize new ATP from ADP and phosphate (P). However, in this case oxygen is absolutely necessary to release energy, no matter if the starting elements of the biochemical reaction are glucose molecules or fatty acids. Atmospheric oxygen is suitably conveyed into the muscles involved in physical exercise, and in particular in the mitochondrions of muscle fibers where it will be properly used.

> glucose + oxygen = carbon dioxide + water + energy
> fatty acids + oxygen = carbon dioxide + water + energy

In soccer, the capability to use as much oxygen in the unit of time as possible, for instance, is very important in order to recover very rapidly after an intense physical effort lasting several seconds (a sprint over a distance of some meters, for example), or after two consecutive efforts of short duration but very close to each other (two consecutive sprints with no pause in between), and so on.

Oxygen debt

Physical effort can also be protracted over a long period of time (several minutes or even hours, in some cases) when muscles use the ATP synthesized through the aerobic mechanism exclusively.

For example, the best 10 km and marathon runners can run 13 mph for several minutes without their blood lactate concentrations increasing. The amount of oxygen conveyed to their muscle tissue and then used by their muscles to carry out specific biochemical reactions is fully exploited to produce a sufficient quantity of ATP to endure physical exercise of such intensity.

On the other hand, if they have to run faster - at a speed of 14 mph, for example - their muscles need to provide more energy and the total amount of ATP produced by the sole aerobic mechanism per minute is no longer enough. Therefore, their muscles must apply to the lactic acid anaerobic mechanism to synthesize the remaining quantity of required ATP - that is the amount beyond the maximal level which can be provided by the aerobic process. However, the activation of the lactic acid anaerobic mechanism inevitably brings about lactic acid production. The athlete can maintain his 14 mph pace no more than a few minutes, that is until his muscle lactic acid (or better, hydrogen ions) concentration becomes so high that it makes the muscles considerably heavy and prevents the runner from maintaining that rhythm. If the athlete ran still faster, his muscles would reach the critical condition much sooner.

The maximal running speed the athlete can maintain over an extended period of time without his blood lactate concentration increasing (this maximal speed is about 12 - 13 mph in the best long-distance runners all over the world) is defined as 'anaerobic threshold'. For a more accurate explanation, in reality blood lactate concentration rises during the first minutes of the running exercise: from standard levels at rest (nearly one millimole per liter of blood) it grows to 4 millimoles per liter on average and then remains unchanged.

The 'anaerobic threshold' speed is a very important index (together with maximal oxygen consumption) of the athlete's anaerobic features. Those soccer players who usually run a lot during the course of a match generally have anaerobic threshold rates close to or even above 11 mph.

The average speed the athlete can maintain while performing the Cooper test (it can be measured by multiplying the distance the athlete covers in 12 minutes by five) nearly corresponds to the anaerobic threshold. In the same way, in many athletes the deflection velocity in the Conconi and Sassi test corresponds to the anaerobic threshold or is very close to it.

Lactic acid debt

In very simple words, the so-called 'lactic acid oxygen debt' (or simply 'lactic acid debt') refers to the total amount of oxygen which would have been necessary to synthesize, through the aerobic mechanism, the same quantity of ATP finally produced by the lactic acid anaerobic process. It is defined as 'oxygen debt' since this process allows the muscles to delay the intake and the utilization of a certain quantity of oxygen. It only acts to postpone it, since - when physical effort decreases to much less intense levels or is completely over - the body must be provided with the amount of oxygen which would have been needed to produce, through the aerobic process, the total quantity of ATP which was then synthesized by the lactic acid anaerobic mechanism and which obviously brought about release of lactic acid. Deep breathing is also evident immediately after strenuous physical exercise since the athlete is in a condition of oxygen debt - for instance, a soccer player covering a 500 or 700 yard distance at a fast pace or immediately after performing the Cooper test.

Badly trained athletes usually recover much more slowly from lactic acid debt conditions. As will be clearly explained in chapter eight (paragraph 8.2.3), it takes about 15 minutes for the athlete to make up the first half of his oxygen deficit; another 15 minutes will be necessary to make up one fourth; another 15 minutes (which means 45 minutes up to now) to replace another eighth of the deficit, and so forth. Therefore, the time the body needs to make up each consecutive half of the whole lactic acid debt is 15 minutes. In well trained athletes who are used to recovering from the debt state very rapidly - which should be the case for professional soccer players - the above-mentioned period of time is normally much shorter and even lower than 7 minutes on some occasions.

Non lactic acid debt

The expression 'non lactic acid oxygen debt' refers to the total amount of ATP the athlete uses up during physical exercise (of short duration, in general) and which was already stored in his muscles or was synthesized through the non lactic acid anaerobic mechanism - or phosphocreatine process. Let's imagine a soccer player who makes a 20 yard sprint immediately after the referee blows the whistle to start the game: his muscles first use up the small amount of ATP which was stored in muscle fibers and then the ATP produced by the non lactic acid anaerobic process, that is the phosphocreatine mechanism. When the sprint is completed, the athlete is in a condition of 'non lactic acid anaerobic debt', since he has drawn on his ATP and phosphocreatine stores. If a pause immediately follows high-intensity exercise (the sprint, in this case), the player can make up that oxygen deficit: this is possible because the body is provided with a suitable amount of oxygen which is used in a chain of aerobic reactions to entirely re-build muscle ATP and phosphocreatine stores up to their original levels. Compared to the lactic acid deficit condition, the recovery from non lactic acid oxygen debt is definitely more rapid. It takes about 30 seconds for non-trained athletes to make up every consecutive half of their oxygen debt, which means that each consecutive half of their original debt is made up every half a minute. In well-trained athletes this period of time is obviously much shorter.

From non lactic acid to lactic acid oxygen debt

Oxygen debt conditions - both lactic acid and non lactic acid - cannot exceed specific maximum levels. It is exactly as if a bank granted a loan to one of its customers, or still better, a series of consecutive small loans and alternated with the return of a certain sum of money, if necessary. The total debt will never exceed a certain level.

As was already explained in the previous paragraphs, the production of ATP through the lactic acid mechanism also brings about the formation of 'waste' products (LA- and H+) and when their muscle concentrations reach certain levels it is almost impossible for the athlete to practice at the same intensity, since his muscles considerably lose their efficiency. The production of this particular amount of 'waste products' corresponds, more or less, to the athlete's maximal lactic acid debt. However, specific training can help muscles to synthesize larger quantities of ATP through the lactic acid mechanism before attaining the critical point: in other words, the athlete's maximal lactic acid debt is very likely to increase by means of suitable athletic conditioning.

As far as non lactic acid oxygen debt is concerned, it is strictly influenced by the total amount of phosphocreatine stored in muscle tissue. Remember that this substance cannot be fully exploited to produce ATP either: only about half of the total quantity can be converted to release energy, while the other 50% cannot be used up. Therefore, let's imagine a soccer player who makes a sprint and consumes a considerable amount of CP (creatine phosphate); as it was explained before, he can gradually replace his CP loss if there is a sufficiently long pause after that high intensity effort. Otherwise, if the athlete is forced to make another sprint or a series of sprints immediately after the first one with no pause in between, his muscles can no longer apply to the non lactic acid energy mechanism and must promptly draw on the lactic acid process once his original phosphocreatine stores have been reduced by nearly 50%. In this way, the body shifts from a condition of non lactic acid debt to a state of lactic acid oxygen deficit: this is exactly what regularly happens during a soccer match.

By simplifying this, during the course of a match - above the total amount of ATP which can be provided by the aerobic mechanism - the athlete's muscles first use up their ATP stores and then promptly apply to non lactic acid ATP. Once the potentially available half of the total non lactic acid ATP is fully exploited, his muscles finally draw on lactic acid ATP to provide energy.

Endurance and the ability to use oxygen in soccer players

On the basis of the previous considerations, the aerobic mechanism plays a crucial role in the recovery phases between two consecutive strenuous efforts. A particularly efficient aerobic mechanism allows the athlete to make up his oxygen debts much more rapidly.

On the other hand, let's suppose that a soccer player has a given oxygen expense per every kilogram of his body weight during the first half of the competition (140 liters in a player whose body weight is 70 kilograms). If his blood lactate concentration corresponds to the maximal lactate concentration in soccer players - that is 14 mmol/l - his lactic acid debt will be 42 ml/kg; if his non lactic acid capacity is very similar to that of a sprinter, his non lactic acid deficit will be 40 ml/kg; therefore, the maximum value of oxygen debt at the end of the first half will be 82 ml/kg, which means 4% of his overall energy expense.

This means that the oxygen debt which accumulates after every lactic acid or non lactic acid physical effort is gradually made up during the course of the competition thanks to the aerobic mechanism.

As to the non lactic acid debt, the re-synthesis of phosphocreatine from elementary molecules - creatine and phosphate (P) - once phosphocreatine itself has released the energy of its 'high energy bond' in order to produce ATP, can be schematically represented as follows:

creatine + P + energy + creatine - - *- - P

The energy appearing on the left side of this biochemical reaction derives from the aerobic process.

The reality becomes much more complex if one wants to clearly explain how the body makes up its lactic acid oxygen debt. In brief, the amount of lactate which forms as a 'waste product' when ATP is synthesized by the lactic acid mechanism completely disappears from the body either because it is broken down to pyruvic acid and then totally burnt to carbon dioxide and water, or because it is removed for conversion to glucose (or glycogen) by the liver. In both cases, it is necessary to provide energy which derives from the aerobic mechanism on this occasion, too.

Furthermore, apart from making up oxygen debts much more rapidly, the aerobic mechanism is of critical importance in soccer, particularly during strenuous exercise. For instance, an outside back who withdraws into his defensive line after taking part in the offensive buildup and runs at a speed of 9 mph, can avoid increasing his oxygen debt (he can even replace part of it) if his anaerobic threshold velocity is 10 or 11 mph. On the contrary, he further boosts his oxygen deficit (or, more easily, maintains a speed considerably slower than 9 mph) if his anaerobic threshold rate is 8 mph.

The Aerobic Components of Energy

As explained in the previous chapter, the presence of oxygen clearly distinguishes the aerobic energy mechanism from the two other energy processes finally leading to the synthesis of ATP, that is the 'fuel' muscle tissue uses to work. From the atmosphere - of which it constitutes about 21% - oxygen is conveyed into muscle fibers, and in mitochondrions in particular, that is the site where combustion takes place to provide energy for the cell's activities. Several biochemical reactions take place in these small corpuscles under the control of a given number of highly specific enzymes. In these biochemical reactions oxygen combines with sugars or fats, or better - for a more accurate description - with the molecules deriving from sugars and fats.

If one wants to analyze all the different phases through which oxygen finally gets into muscle tissue:

- when breathing in, oxygen penetrates into the body through the mouth or the nose, passes through some important organs such as the windpipe, the bronchial tubes and the bronchioles, enters the lungs and finally reaches those very small cavities, the air sacs, better known as pulmonary alveoli;
- once they reach the pulmonary alveoli, oxygen molecules penetrate through some membranes and enter the blood stream, where they bind to hemoglobin, the red pigment of the blood;
- hemoglobin consists of a protein - globin - and an iron compound - 'haem' - and is carried by the red blood cells;
- the blood is kept in constant motion by the heart (which acts as a pump); therefore, the red blood cells can carry oxygen through increasingly thin tubes and cavities and convey it to the whole body; in this way, muscle tissue is also provided with the

suitable amount of oxygen;
- in the smallest blood vessels (the capillaries) - which are present in very large numbers in muscle tissue and have extremely thin membranes - oxygen separates from hemoglobin, penetrates through the capillaries' membranes and finally enters muscle fibers;
- once it gets into the muscle fiber, oxygen combines with myoglobin, an oxygen-carrying pigment in muscle, somehow similar to hemoglobin; it is this particular molecule which finally carries oxygen into the mitochondrions.

In order to better understand all the various training methods, it could be useful for a coach to distinguish two main components characterizing the aerobic energy mechanism:
- the central aerobic components, by which oxygen is carried into muscle tissue ('oxygen intake');
- the peripheral aerobic components, through which muscles can use a more or less high percentage of the oxygen conveyed to muscle tissue ('oxygen consumption').

Central aerobic components
When speaking of central aerobic components in soccer, the reference is typically made to muscles' oxygen intake - as explained in the previous paragraph - and this specifically concerns those muscle groups which are most involved in the movements characterized particularly in soccer, mainly concerning the lower limb muscles.

What is the real reason why oxygen intake by those particular muscles is high in some individuals and low in others? Of all the various systems, organs and tissues which take part in constantly providing muscles with the suitable amount of oxygen they need, which one can be considered the weakest link in the chain? In other words, what is the real factor limiting the maximum amount of oxygen which can be conveyed to muscle tissue per second?

Even though in the last few years researchers have realized that, in some persons, some particular ventilation components are of critical importance in cases of high-intensity exercise, the total amount of air our lungs breathe in and out per minute is very unlikely to represent a crucial element reducing muscle maximal oxygen intake in young and well-trained soccer players.

The release of oxygen from alveolar air (that is the air filling up pulmonary alveoli) to the blood is also unlikely to reduce muscle maximal oxygen intake. On the contrary, the blood can play a cru-cial role in this context. An increasing number of athletes in differ-ent sports disciplines suffer from anemia due to sports activity today, mainly because too often the gradual increase in training loads is not combined with a suitable and rational diet, and this can obvi-ously cause serious imbalances between the 'intake' and the 'loss' of iron from the body. However, in general most people tend to believe that the blood is not responsible for reducing muscle oxy-gen intake in non-anemic players. The total volume of blood flow-ing in the body of a well-trained athlete is much larger than that of an individual who has the same body weight but practices no sports activity. Some particular training methods work to bring about a more sensible increase in the total volume of the blood.

Moreover, people tend to attach greater importance to the car-diac output. That is the total volume of blood which is pumped per minute. The cardiac output results from the stroke volume (the total amount of blood expelled at each heart contraction) multiplied by the heart rate (the number of heart contractions per minute). As I already underlined, there are two fundamental indicators of the level of an athlete's aerobic features, that is his maximal oxygen con-sumption and his anaerobic threshold. Notice that various athletes can have completely different aerobic levels, but the same identical heart rates when they reach their maximal oxygen consumption or anaerobic thresholds while undertaking a specific test. This could help us understand that the heart rate does not act as a factor lim-iting the volume of blood which can be conveyed to the whole body. The real limiting factor is the cardiac output, i.e. the volume of blood that the heart can expel from the left ventricle and pump into the aorta for distribution around the body each time it beats at full rhythm.

There are some particular training methods which are highly effective to enhance the cardiac output; paragraph 7.1 will deal with their specific features.

Peripheral aerobic components

Once the blood is pumped to the muscles actively involved in phys-ical exercise, muscle fibers must also be provided with the suitable amount in the best way possible. There must be suitable conditions for the oxygen to leave the capillaries, enter the muscle fibers and finally reach the mitochondrions where it is exploited to release energy.

The distribution of the blood to muscle fibers strictly depends on a sufficient density of capillaries around the muscle fibers involved in the particular kind of activity one is practicing; jogging (which was defined as 'capillarization exercise' in the past) enhances the increase in the number of capillaries only around type I muscle fibers, also known as 'red' or 'slowly-conducting' fibers (STF fibers). On the other hand, high-intensity running exercise should also cause an increase in the density of capillaries around type II muscle fibers, or 'pale' or 'fast-conducting' muscle fibers (FTF fibers). The process by which new capillaries form around muscle fibers is much less complicated than it was thought to be in the past.

As to oxygen intake by muscle fibers and its real use, with the exception of those players who are obliged to stop practicing for a period of time, these mechanisms are strictly connected to myoglobin activity (myglobin acts as a sort of shuttle, by carrying oxygen from muscle fibers' membranes to mitochondrions), but specifically to the activity of the enzymes present in mitochondrions and responsible for catalyzing the chain of biochemical reactions for the controlled combustion of the molecules deriving from sugars, fats and proteins (in a small percentage).

Therefore, the most effective training methods for the definite improvement of peripheral aerobic components are those which are specifically based on running exercise at a speed very close to anaerobic threshold (for further details see paragraph 6.1)

Training Peripheral Aerobic Components

The expression 'peripheral aerobic components' refers to the ability of muscles (those muscle groups involved in the specific physical activity; the lower limb muscles in soccer) to take up large amounts of oxygen per second. In this context, the activity of mitochondrial enzymes plays a role of crucial importance, since they catalyze those biochemical reactions where oxygen combines together with sugar and fat molecules (in the specific case of soccer, it mainly combines with sugar molecules) to release the energy necessary to synthesize ATP, that is the 'fuel', the sole possible source of energy that muscles can use to work.

6.1 The main features of the stimulus enhancing peripheral aerobic components

Significant advances have been made in training peripheral aerobic components and the situation is definitely favorable today. The modern knowledge on this subject allows researchers to clearly identify the most effective basic stimulus for enhancing such important components.

Benzi and his team's researches proved that a small amount of lactate must be produced and stored in muscle tissue to enhance the activity of mitochondrial enzymes (and thus improve peripheral aerobic components).

This could even sound paradoxical: one could wonder how is it possible to involve the lactic acid mechanism to enhance the aerobic mechanism by means of regular training?

By simplifying the reality, in many biological processes it is first of all necessary to upset the enzyme system itself to finally enhance its effectiveness. When speaking of 'upsetting' the aerobic mechanism I mean reaching such an intensity at which the sole aerobic process no longer suffices to synthesize the suitable amount of ATP and the lactic acid mechanism must therefore be promptly activated to satisfy those needs.

From a more practical point of view, a very slow running speed which does not cause lactic acid to store in muscles and even be produced in minimum amounts (which means a fully aerobic running speed) is definitely useless to enhance aerobic features - with the exception of very unfit athletes. This is why it is advisable to practice at a slightly higher intensity and speed. The athlete should run at a speed very close to his anaerobic threshold or, better, slightly above it, that is from 100% to 105% of the anaerobic threshold itself.

Moreover, I would like to highlight another fundamental quality for the training stimulus to be really effective: it must last for several seconds, at least. If an athlete starts from a standing position and undertakes 700 yard repetition running at a very constant pace, it takes several seconds for him to reach a perfect oxygen balance. During the first minute the mechanisms responsible for carrying oxygen from the lungs to the muscles - those of the cardiovascular system, in particular - are not at their top efficiency levels yet. The heart rate, for instance, is still increasing and, moreover, muscle fibers are using up the small amount of oxygen stored in myoglobin. This starting phase in which the body cannot reach a condition of perfect balance is definitely useful and has a training nature from other points of view, but cannot have the same positive effects on mitochondrial enzymes. Their activity will be best enhanced only later, after the first starting minute, when the body is in a condition of oxygen balance. If we want to be absolutely accurate in our description, the athlete cannot reach a real balance in the interval between the first minute after the start and the end of the 700 meter repetition, since some particular parameters constantly change. Others, on the contrary, gradually become more constant, such as the heart rate, or the volume of oxygen conveyed to muscles per second, or the percentage of that oxygen used by muscle tissue, or the amount of lactic acid produced per second.

This is why I am firmly convinced that what I usually define as 'aerobic repetitions' are the best training methods to enhance the athlete's peripheral aerobic components - even though there are undoubtedly some other ways to improve these qualities. In order to avoid any misunderstanding, I would like to underline that the most typical among those conditioning methods are the 500 and

700 yard repetitions and that they are not defined 'aerobic' only because they involve the aerobic mechanism (like in very slow running), but because there is a definite improvement in peripheral aerobic components as a result of the activation of the lactic acid mechanism.

Remember that the running repetitions made over short distances, at such an intensity which brings about the production of considerable amounts of lactate and in a long interval of time (200 yard repetitions, for instance) do not train peripheral aerobic components. According to some important researchers, this kind of exercise would even have a negative effect on them. On the basis of my observations directly on the field - this inhibiting effect does not exist at all, provided that the athlete's peripheral aerobic components are constantly stimulated according to the most suitable training criteria (in the same week training cycle, for instance).

Aerobic repetitions

As a consequence of what was explained in paragraph 6.1, the most effective stimulus for the soccer player to really improve his peripheral aerobic components is running exercise with the following characteristics:

- **a speed:** very close to the athlete's anaerobic threshold velocity (or slightly faster);
- **duration:** the athlete runs for an extended period of time (more than several seconds, at least).

As a result of my personal experience, I tend to prefer running repetitions over distances of several hundreds yards - 700 yards in particular - at a speed which is 3 to 5% above the anaerobic threshold velocity. Obviously, there are some other suitable methods for the final improvement of peripheral aerobic components, for instance those shown in table 6.1 and in the paragraphs 6.3 and 13.6. However, I think that soccer players should mainly practice 700 yard running repetitions (or very similar distances) during the pre-season training period - and also during the soccer season, by combining this workout with other training exercises.

Preliminary workouts

Aerobic repetitions and all the other training methods specifically aimed at enhancing peripheral aerobic components can be performed properly and without completely tiring out the body only if the athlete has already experienced a basic conditioning phase.

Table 6.1
The most typical training methods to enhance peripheral aerobic components.
The most suitable stimulus for the soccer player to finally improve his peripheral aerobic components is undoubtedly running. However, the athlete must run:
- at a speed which is very close to his anaerobic threshold velocity, which means it brings about the production and the storage of small amounts of lactic acid;
- over a sufficiently extended period of time (more than several seconds, at least).

From this point of view, the training methods which are supposed to best enhance those important qualities are:
1. Running repetitions:
1.1 over a distance of 400 to 750 yards with timing, the time is set and varies according the single player's aerobic features;
1.2 over non-accurately measured and/or non-timed distances.
2. One single repetition at a regular pace:
2.1 'short and fast' of 10 to 15 minutes;
2.2 Cooper Test (12 minutes) and other tests for set time or distance, like 3,000 meter run test and similar.
3. Fartlek running, that is running with speed variations ('stimuli') at set times (every 30 seconds, preferably) or distances (100 yards, at least):
3.1 one single repetition of 15 to 20 minutes at least;
3.2 two or more repetitions of 10 minutes each.
4. Short aerobic repetitions (150 to 200 meters) at very short intervals often, even shorter than 50 seconds.

Soccer players generally practice by themselves while on vacation. Their personal training plans usually include running at least, so that they can start their pre-season conditioning in good shape.

Moreover, they have already run many (even hundreds of) miles during their career and many of them have also done aerobic repetitions. All this obviously helps the player when he must run 700 meter aerobic repetitions (the conditioning plan can also include shorter or longer distances) at the beginning of the pre-season training period.

This is why soccer players usually need very few preliminary training sessions (three, for instance) the first days of their pre-season training camp; these sessions could be planned as follows:

first day: 10 to 15 min. stretch and mobility; 25 to 35 min. running, (the speed increases gradually from very slow to high-intensity running); 3 to 5 changes of pace of about 15 to 30 seconds each during the last 10 minutes; while changing the pace, the speed rises considerably, but cannot prevent the athlete from maintaining a very relaxed way of running;

second day: 10 to 15 min. stretch and mobility; 35 to 45 min. running by gradually increasing the speed while also including 4 to 5 changes of pace of about 30 to 45 seconds each during the last 15 minutes; three 300 to 400 yard running repetitions with the players divided into 3 or 4 groups (if the fitness coach does not know the aerobic features of each player yet, the players can be divided into different groups according to their running abilities); the coach times the repetitions but the players are not asked to cover the distance in a set time;

third day: 10 to 15 min. stretch and mobility; 10 min. running; 4 - 100 yard sprinting repetitions; 1 X 150 to 200 yard sprinting repetition; a test to properly assess the players' aerobic fitness (Conconi and Sassi test or Cooper test or 3,000 meter run test).

It is advisable to increase the number of preliminary conditioning sessions for those players who have not trained suitably while on vacation. Most of or all those preliminary sessions should include running with specific features:

- the intensity of physical exercise should vary progressively through gradual changes of pace (the duration should increase session by session) and/or uphill and downhill running; the basic rhythm should become increasingly faster as miles go by.

It would be advisable for athletes to go running in a natural environment, turning about from time to time to wait for the latecomers if necessary.

However, I firmly believe that the test for aerobic fitness should be made at the very beginning of the pre-season training period so as to properly assess the players' basic condition and therefore have a reference to measure the progress they have made during the course of the soccer season.

The suitable place for running repetitions

Running repetitions should be practiced on a perfectly measured ground, with a smooth surface (so as to favor good contact of the feet with the ground and reduce the risk of injuries to minimum levels) and curves as 'rounded off' as possible. Most coaches use the same track for Conconi and Sassi, Cooper or 3,000 meter running tests. Common running tracks are very good, even though some coaches still prefer to avoid the coherent materials which they are typically covered with and therefore suggest their players to run inside the curb, directly on the grass (in this case, every lap is slightly shorter than the standard 400 meters).

If the coach decides to use the playing field, he can mark out a grassy track 300 meters long (or even a bit longer). For instance, it can correspond to one third of a mile if there is enough room to run behind the goals and outside the field's boundaries. It is possible to delimit the curves by using a series of upright posts standing very close to each other (about one yard apart). If the posts must be removed every day, it is advisable to mark the points where they must be set the next time - by using spray paint.

I would like to insist on the real importance of properly measuring the area where running repetitions (and all the tests for aerobic fitness) are made. It is advisable to use suitable specific measuring tapes. When the training plan includes the same repetitions and players run along the same grassy track for some days, their footprints are evident on the ground, the track is already marked out and it can be measured again only if necessary.

Choosing and controlling the speed of aerobic repetitions

If the coach chooses the Conconi and Sassi Test, it is quite easy to set the speed at which players should run the 1,000 meter aerobic repetitions: it is necessary to refer to the deflection speed and increase it by 3 to 5 % (table 6.2). In the early stages of the pre-season period - players are also allowed to run at their threshold velocity.

In the case of the Cooper test or the 3,000 meter running test, the coach can refer to table 6.3 and table 6.4 in order to easily assess the times for 1,000 meter aerobic repetitions. If the coach chooses one of those run tests for set time or distance, he should measure the time taken by every athlete every 1,000 meters (or even every 500 meters). Moreover, in those cases (which are quite common in soccer) where the physical effort is not uniformly distributed in time -- that is in the case of either a too fast start followed by a gradual decrease, or a too cautious start and an excessively fast end - the coach should suggest set times which are a few seconds shorter than those he can get from the tables below. For example, the athletes who cover a distance of 3,000 meters in 12 minutes (which means 1,000 meters every 4 minutes on average), but maintain a pace below 3 min. 45 sec. while running the first or last 1000 meters should not be suggested the right time specifically appearing in the tables 6.3 and 6.4 for those who run 3,000 meters in 12 minutes (that is 3 min. 45 sec.): the most suitable time with a uniform pace would be 3 min. 40 sec. to 3 min. 42 sec.

Dv (deflection velocity) (km/h)	Speed (mph) Over a 1,000 meter distance dv x 1.00 - 1.05	Times (min. and sec.) of the 1,000 meter
13	13.6 - 13.65	4'37" - 4'24"
13.5	13.5 - 14.17	4'20" - 4'14"
14	14.0 - 14.7	4'17" - 4'05"
14.5	14.5 - 15.22	4'08 - 3'56"
15	15.0 - 15.75	4'00" - 3'48"
15.5	15.5 - 16.27	3'52" - 3'41"
16	16.0 - 16.80	3'45" - 3'34"
16.5	16.5 - 17.32	3'38" - 3'28"
17	17.0 - 17.85	3'32" - 3'22"
17.5	17.5 - 18.37	3'26" - 3'16"
18	18.0 - 18.90	3'20" - 3'10"
18.5	18.5 - 19.42	3'15" - 3'05"
19	19.0 - 19.95	3'09" - 3'00"

Table 6.2 - From the Conconi and Sassi Test to the times of the 1,000 meter repetitions
For deflection velocities between 13 and 19 km/h, the table shows the most effective speed patterns (second column, in km/h) and times (third column, in minutes and seconds) for the final improvement of peripheral aerobic components, in 1,000 meter running repetitions. The reference is made to the deflection velocity (dv) measured for every single player in the Conconi and Sassi test.

Once the coach clearly assesses the ideal pace every single player should maintain over a given distance (table 6.5 shows the times over 500, 600 and 800 meter distances which correspond to those over 1,000 meters), he should divide the players into 3 or 4 groups, each one characterized by similar goals as to the set times for running repetitions. The players should therefore respect the set times the coach suggests to them and work to maintain their regular pace. For this to be possible, the players should be given the possibility of comparing their times when covering set distances - 150, 300 and 450 meters if the track is 300 meters long, for instance; or 200, 400 and 600 meters if the track is 400 meters long. Intermediate distances should therefore be accurately shown. Furthermore, for each group of players there should be a person (the coach, the fitness coach, the goalkeeper coach, an injured player and so forth...) who is responsible for timing the athletes and comparing their real times with the ideal ones - which were previously measured and then written on a chart - so that he can immediately inform them if they are ahead or behind and how big the gap is.

There is another method for players to constantly keep their running pace under control: one player in each group should have a stopwatch and know the ideal times at set distances. Maintaining a regular speed (as far as 200 to 300 meters before the finishing line, at least; those who still have enough energy could even increase their speed at that point) definitely helps the athlete to cover the distance in a set time more easily and also has better conditioning effects.

6.2.4 How the coach should revise the times he suggests to his players

The coach should not be excessively strict and expect his players to perfectly respect set times in the first training sessions (including aerobic exercise). On the contrary, he should be absolutely reasonable and allow his players - specifically those who are not used to performing this kind of physical exercise - to practice according to their own conditioning level.

However, session by session players should be asked to work increasingly harder. Aerobic repetitions bring about a rapid increase in the anaerobic threshold; in young athletes it can increase by 2 mph or more after 8 to 10 training sessions and only seldom does it rise by less than 1 mph, even in 'old' athletes. Therefore, it would be a great mistake to ask the players to always run aerobic repetitions in the same interval of time, since they would run the risk of maintaining a too slow speed for aerobic exercise to have its best conditioning effects.

Athletes usually realize they are improving their running times almost naturally. Apart from technical and psychological adjustments and variations, they also experience a gradual improvement from the aerobic point of view and necessarily run faster if their sense of fatigue remains unchanged.

However, since the anaerobic mechanism can be constantly enhanced only if it is involved in physical exercise, it is necessary to regularly and gradually adjust training plans to the players constant improvements - only in this way can the coach be sure that lactic acid in his players' muscles are sufficient to activate the anaerobic process. Since players obviously cannot go through continuous testing, the coach should constantly refer to the accurate analysis of the times taken by his players while performing aerobic repetitions (which should be considered as tests, in practice!) in order to regularly adjust his conditioning plans. This is why the times taken by every single player in every aerobic repetition should be taken accurately.

On the other hand, it is obvious that for those players who can easily maintain the pace expected of them and even run set distances in much better times than expected because they gain time per lap and/or increase their speed in the final part of the track, the coach should set new times which are a few seconds shorter than the previous ones in the following session. It is also advisable to suggest a slight increase - specifically in the first training sessions including aerobic exercise - to those who have maintained the speed expected of them.

Nevertheless, the coach should always comply with specific criteria: first of all, he should set a time for each player which is generally a few seconds shorter than the value he gets by finding the average of the various times taken in the previous session (the worst should always be excluded); briefly, he should average the three best times if there have been four trials, or the four best trials out of five and so on, and then subtract a few seconds so as to include the player in one of three or four groups.

As to the time the coach should set for each player, it is probably better to underline that while some tables (table 6.5 in particular) show very accurate values, coaches should always use rounded off figures.

The number of running repetitions and recovery time

Pre-season training plans usually include aerobic repetitions every two days alternated with uphill running. After the three or four preliminary sessions which I clearly dealt with in paragraph 6.2.1 (the third session should include either the Conconi and Sassi test or the Cooper test), the coach can immediately plan real running repetitions with accurate timing: one set of three 800 meter repetitions (3 x 800m) the first time, which must be immediately replaced by 1,000 meter repetitions. If players are asked to cover such distances at a speed 3 to 5% faster than their anaerobic threshold velocity, the practice plan cannot include too many repetitions at a time, since it also includes other conditioning workouts and technical and tactical work as well.

As far as the recovery time between two consecutive repetitions is concerned, it should not be shorter than the repetition itself. In general, I suggest a pause of about 4 to 4 1/2 minutes between the first and the second repetition which could even rise to 5 minutes in the following intervals if I see that some players need more time to recover from fatigue. For conditioning to be really effective, it is much more useful to keep the quality of exercise at high levels rather than reduce the recovery interval. In brief, the stimulus is fundamental and should bring about all the expected changes. The recovery interval between two consecutive repetitions is of minor importance in this particular kind of work.

6.3 Aerobic repetitions during the soccer season and possible alternative solutions

From the psychological point of view, it is almost impossible for players to be highly stimulated and motivated if they know they are going to run four or five 1,000 meter repetitions on a given track and in a set time every Tuesday throughout the season. On the other hand, specific training for peripheral aerobic components is absolutely useful, since it helps players to maintain their best physical efficiency throughout the soccer season. Therefore, coaches should work on alternative solutions to the most typical aerobic practice (such as dividing their players into 3 or 4 groups according to the standard pre-season training methods, such as accurate timing, set times, information about the time at set distances and so forth...). For instance, they could:

Results of the Copper test (meters in 12 min)	Time which should be suggested for 1,000 meter repetitions
3600	3'05"
3500	3'10"
3400	3'16"
3300	3'23"
3200	3'30"
3100	3'37"
3000	3'45"
2900	3'53"
2800	4'02"
2700	4'12"
2600	4'22"
2500	4'33"
2400	4'55"

Table 6.3 - From the Cooper Test to the times over 1,000 meter distances. The times that the coach should suggest for 1,000 meter running repetitions in relation to the Cooper Test's results: professional players were accurately studied to get such information.

Time taken to cover 3,000 meters	Time which should be suggested for 1,000 meter repetitions
10'	3.05"
10'15"	3'10"
10'30"	3'15"
10'45"	3'20"
11'	3'25"
11'15"	3'30"
11'30"	3'35"
11'45"	3'40"
12'	3'45"
12'15"	3'50"
12'30"	3'55"
12'45"	4'
13'	4'0"
13'15"	4'10"
13'30"	4'15"
13'45"	4'20"
14'	4'25"
14'15"	4'30"
14'30"	4'35"
14'45"	4'40"
15'	4'45"

Table 6.4 - From the 3,000 meters test to the times over 1,000 meter distances. The times that the coach should suggest for 1,000 meter running repetitions, in relation to the 3,000 meters test's results.

- **vary environmental conditions:** take players for practice in a park, in a wood or so forth. Many years ago, I took my players of Varese Club to the nearby golf course in Luvinate and told them to run to one particular tree, turn around and run back to the starting place. They covered a distances 1,000 yards and even more, and the training effect was the same, but the players felt as if they were performing a completely different exercise.
- **group players of varying speeds:** ask the players to perform a sort of 'chase' 1,000 meter repetitions; instead of selecting players of similar level to form the various groups, each team consist of athletes who usually cover the same distance in

completely different times. For instance, in a group consisting of a player who runs 1,000 meters in 3 min 10 sec, the second in 3 min 22 sec and the third in 3 min 35 sec - the latter starts first, the second starts 13 seconds later (this is exactly the difference between 3 min. 35 sec and 3 min 22 sec) and the former sprints 25 seconds later. If the three players all maintain their natural pace, they will finish the repetition simultaneously;

- **vary the distances of the aerobic repetitions**, for instance 800 meters (5 x 800 m), 600 meters (5 or 6 repetitions x 600m), or combine different distances by choosing various solutions: the length of the track can either gradually increase (400m + 500m + 600m + 700m + 800m) or decrease (1,200m + 1,000m + 800m + 600m + 400m) or have a pyramidal structure with a gradual increase to reach a peak distance and finally decrease (500m + 600m + 800m + 1,000m + 800m + 600m + 500m) and so forth. In this sense, the coach can obviously choose a number of different solutions, but must pay great attention to the times - table 6.5 could be a very useful reference.

- **decide on one single test**: use one of the specific run tests for set time (Cooper test - 12 min) or distance (3,000 meters, for example) - time and distance can also vary according to the coach's needs;

- **plan much shorter repetitions with very short recovery intervals** (I define them as 'short aerobic repetitions') use distances such as 300 or even 250 meters (for instance, 2 sets of 5 x 300m or 3 sets of 4 x 250m), but with very short recovery intervals, below 50 seconds. The player should run such distances at a slightly faster speed than in 500 or 600 meter repetitions. Such a short recovery interval would not cause his heart rate to fall to rest levels and the athlete is very likely to be in the ideal condition for enhancing his peripheral aerobic components within a very short time (20 sec to 30 sec) from the start of the 250 - 300 meter repetition. When I first introduced this kind of aerobic exercise, most players enjoyed it.

- **introduce running with changes of pace (usually referred to as 'Fartlek')**; the players run all together and the basic pace is generally slower than the anaerobic threshold velocity of the weakest player, while - during the various change-of-pace phases (stimul) - it corresponds to or is even faster than the speed players are expected to maintain while running 500 or 600 meter repetitions. For each stimulus to be really effective, it should last at least 30 to 40 seconds. The decrease in the heart rate (and in the other parameters) is smaller than in the previous exercise and, therefore, it generally takes a much shorter time for the body to restore the ideal conditions for the final improvement of peripheral aerobic components. In this case too, the coach can work on a number of different solutions: he can suggest such exercises as 2 repetitions of 12 minutes with stimuli of 40 seconds each every 3 minutes; or 24 minutes with changes of pace of 30, 40, 50, 60 seconds with double recovery intervals; or 15 minutes combining one minute of slow running and one minute of sprinting and so forth. Remember that, for this kind of exercise (Fartlek) to be really effective in enhancing peripheral aerobic components, the duration of each stimulus must be short, the interval between two consecutive stimuli must be minimal, and the basic pace must be fast. Although players usually like this exercise, it is difficult for the coach to keep the athlete's speed under constant control.

Chapter 13 (paragraph 13.6, in particular) will specifically focus the attention on the training methods which can be used during the course of the soccer season to enhance aerobic components and peripheral components, in particular.

1000 m	800 m	600 m	500 m
2'50"	2'10" 5	1'33" 7	1'14" 6
3'00"	2'18"	1'39" 4	1'19" 2
3'10"	2'55" 5	1'45" 1	1'23" 8
3'20"	2'33"	1'50" 8	1'28" 4
3'30"	2'40" 5	1'56" 5	1'33" 1
3'40"	2'48"	2'02" 2	1'37" 8
3'50"	2'55" 5	2'07" 9	1'42" 5
4'	3'03"	2'13" 6	1'47" 2

Table 6.5 - Equivalence between the times over 1,000 meters and other distances
Equivalence between the times taken to cover 1,000 meters (first column) and those taken to cover 800, 600 and 500 meter distances. Remember that these equivalences cannot perfectly suit some players. The table shows very accurate times for 800, 600 and 500 meter distances since these are the perfect equivalences with the times over 1,000 meters. The coach should obviously round off the values he is going to suggest to his players. I usually suggest beginning with 3 repetitions and gradually increasing to 4 (starting from the second training week, in general) and 5 (after two or three sessions specifically dedicated to this exercise); I believe that only those players with good basic cardiovascular endurance (and who are also highly motivated) can run 6 1,000 meter repetitions at a speed which is 5% faster than that of their anaerobic threshold, without overlooking other kinds of exercise at the same time.

7

Training Central Aerobic Components

As pointed out in the fifth chapter, the expression 'central aerobic components' refers to the oxygen intake by the working muscles directly involved in the physical effort. That chapter also explained that - all other conditions being equal - the most important factor which directly influences muscle oxygen intake in a certain individual is the capacity of his or her heart to 'pump' a large volume of blood per minute.

I believe that it is also absolutely fundamental for soccer coaches and experts to clearly understand that the most specific stimulus for enhancing central aerobic components does not correspond to the more specific impulse for the final improvement of peripheral aerobic mechanisms. Obviously, there are some particular methods which somehow train both peripheral and central aerobic components, but it is much better to distinguish and try to apply the most specific ones.

The main features of the stimulus enhancing central aerobic components

I think that the most effective stimulus for the final improvement of central aerobic components is physical exercise involving a sudden increase in the heart rate. Uphill sprinting repetitions over distances of several meters are the most effective training method for this sudden increase.

In 1978-79 I was the fitness coach of the Under 18 team of Varese soccer Club. Together with coach Eugenio Fascetti, I began to plan the pre-season conditioning period so as to regularly include uphill running repetitions. With that kind of exercise we mostly intended to work on the athletes' lactic acid mechanisms. We strongly believed that uphill sprinting repetitions caused players to produce larger amounts of lactic acid than in the same physical exercise carried out on level ground.

After a very short time, Fascetti and I realized that the conditioning method we were using was highly beneficial. The players were generally in much better physical condition when they had to play pre-season matches. For instance, they had no serious difficulties when accelerating, as had usually happened when we used lactic acid exercises on level ground (for further details on the subject, see paragraph 7.3.2). Moreover, the results of the tests helped us to realize that there had been remarkable improvements from the aerobic point of view and such improvements could not be completely explained as the direct effect of the aerobic repetitions made until then.

By measuring the heart rate of the players during uphill sprinting repetitions (just a bit more than 70 meters long with a one in five gradient on average), we realized how sudden the increase in the heart rate really was: from about 100 heartbeats per minute at the end of the recovery interval between two consecutive repetitions it rose to or even above 180 heartbeats per minute within the 12 seconds of the uphill track.

Prof. Reindell, the German physiologist who more than anybody else studied the so-called standard interval training which typically consisted of sets of 200 meter repetitions with recovery intervals of 45 sec to 90 sec, during which the heart rate usually fell to nearly 120 heartbeats per minute. In order to clearly explain the real benefits of that conditioning method, Prof. Reindell pointed out that while running the first part of the 200 meter repetition, the athlete experiences a very rapid increase in his heart rate and this is exactly the most important stimulus for finally enhancing the capacity of the heart to 'pump' larger volumes of blood.

But let's go back to soccer questions. As I said before, Eugenio Fascetti and I gradually realized that uphill running repetitions brought about a sudden increase in the heart rate and that such increase was much quicker than in running repetitions on level ground. Therefore, according to Reindell's theories, that kind of physical exercise was expected to enhance cardiovascular endurance in a much more effective way. This is why I began to focus my attention on a small number of amateur long-distance runners whose training plan was based on running exclusively (40 to 60 km a week). I slightly modified their conditioning plans so as to include some uphill repetitions in two training sessions a week, while the overall duration of physical exercise remained unchanged. I found out that this caused an increase in maximal oxygen intake.

I also discovered - even though indirectly, (from the drop in the total number of heartbeats necessary for an equal increase in the running speed on level ground to be possible) - that the heart seemed to 'pump' a larger volume of blood per heartbeat.

Uphill running repetitions

According to my personal experience, uphill sprinting repetitions are highly effective if they are made over distances of at least 60 meters, with a gradient of more than 15%. If the gradient is smaller, it is advisable to increase the distance (to 70 meters, at least). The duration of top-intensity exercise should be at least 9 seconds at least. It is important to accurately choose the ground so as to avoid any problem in the contact of the feet. Asphalt is very good also because the impact of the body on the ground at the end of the air phase is not so traumatic as the impact on a level ground - for further details, see paragraph 7.4.

At the very beginning of the pre-season training period the coach should arrange some preliminary workouts:

3 or 4 - 40 to 45 meter uphill sprinting repetitions with a recovery interval of about 1 min 30 sec between two consecutive repetitions, at the end of the session which already includes fitness training or technical and tactical exercises - this work can also be suggested on the fourth or fifth day of the pre-season period;

4 to 6 - 50 to 55 meter uphill repetitions with a recovery interval of about 1 min 30 sec to 2 min, always at the end of a training session mainly based on other exercises, one or two days after the previous one.

During the course of the first pre-season training week uphill sprinting exercise can be included in the pre-season conditioning plan. In general, shifting from 40 to 45 meter uphill repetitions to 50 to 55 meter repetitions considerably increases the athlete's sense of fatigue. Such an increase is still more evident when shifting to 60 to 70 meter uphill sprints since each extra meter seems dreadfully heavy!

This first training session including uphill repetitions over full distances (60 to 70 meters) could be planned as follows:

2 sets of 3 repetitions, with a recovery interval of about 3 minutes between two consecutive repetitions, and 4 to 5 minutes between the two sets.

As to the recovery time, I would include running in that interval:

in practice, I asked my players to cover the distance from the peak to the foot of the slope by running slowly following a path through the woods or something similar. Now, I ask my athletes to walk from the peak to the foot of the slope and then wait for the whole recovery interval to elapse. Not only should the recovery interval allow a suitable amount of lactic acid to leave muscle tissue and enter the blood stream, but it should also help the heart rate to lower sensibly. In short, the recovery pause should be reasonably long. Since this particular physical exercise is aimed at causing sudden acceleration in the heart rate (as explained in paragraph 7.1), the heart rate itself should be rather low when starting each uphill sprinting repetition. If the players can use one or more suitable devices for measuring the heart rate while practicing physical exercise, I would suggest the following approximate values:

- the heart rate should be close to 100 heartbeats per minute or below this value at the start of every uphill repetition of each set; it can gradually increase - but should never exceed 120 to 125 heartbeats per minute - at the start of all the other running repetitions.

As to the progression of uphill running repetitions in the pre-season period, considering that it is advisable to introduce a different session I would suggest the following conditioning progression:
- first session: 2 sets of 3 repetitions each;
- second session: 2 sets of 4 repetitions;
- third session: 3 sets of 4 repetitions;
- fourth session: 3 sets of 5 repetitions;
- fifth session: 3 sets of 6 repetitions;
- sixth and seventh sessions: 4 sets of 5 repetitions;
- eighth and ninth sessions: 5 sets of 5 repetitions;
- tenth session: 6 sets of 5 repetitions.

A session like the last one (6 sets of 5 repetitions each) is undoubtedly very demanding for players: moreover, if we also include both warm up and warm down, it generally lasts nearly two hours and this inevitably involves great physical and psychological stress. Only on very rare occasions and with highly motivated athletes could I plan more exercise in one single session (7 sets of 5 repetitions).

For youth players, 4 or 5 sets of 5 repetitions are a very effective exercise. Obviously, the gradient and the length of the slope, as well as the progression in the total number of uphill repetitions between two consecutive sessions also cause considerable differences in the level of fatigue. Furthermore, when the coach times his athletes in all the running repetitions, their physical efforts tend to increase to top levels and they try to run at full speed until the end. This is unlikely to happen if there is no timing of the repetitions. Therefore, the coach should assess whether it is worthwhile timing his players in relation to the situation.

Headache, nausea and vomiting can develop in those players who have never performed uphill running. This is why pre-training diet also plays a crucial role in this context: the meal immediately preceding the training session (remember that there must always be enough time for players to digest between the end of the meal and the beginning physical practice) should not be too generous and the foods which are difficult to digest should be completely avoided - therefore, it is advisable to avoid drinking white coffee if the morning training session includes uphill running repetitions! For more information on training diets 'Nutrition for Soccer Players' is a thorough resource. Great attention must also be focused on the warm up. Such sickness is specifically due to the fact that large production of lactic acid by the muscles directly causes a decrease in blood pH levels (which means that acidity rises) and this affects the central nervous system. It has been my experience that those players who have more powerful muscle mass and greater explosiveness usually suffer most from these general disorders, since they are more likely to produce larger amounts of lactic acid than their fellow players. However, general disorders typically appear in the first sessions exclusively and the physical adaptation to the production of larger amounts of hydrogen ions seems to be very rapid.

The main effects of uphill running repetitions

If on one hand the prompt increase in the heart rate is of crucial importance in enhancing central aerobic components, on the other side running uphill repetitions are specifically beneficial for soccer players from other points of view. First of all, every uphill repetition causes muscles to produce a certain amount of lactic acid. Such lactic acid production could also result from other physical exercise (for further details see chapter eight), in particular by running such distances on level ground in which physical effort is protracted for similar periods of time - 80 to 100 meters, for example.

However, according to my personal experience, at the very beginning of the pre-season period soccer players often fail to run on level ground and maintain the same physical and psychological effort they would have while performing uphill running. Players typically take very long steps while running at full speed on level ground and hardly overwork their muscles to top levels (in order to avoid hurting their hamstrings, in particular), specifically if their muscle tissue is still 'poisoned' by the exercise carried out in the previous sessions. On the contrary, such a wide stride is not prerequisite for the standard biomechanical movements made in uphill running. Moreover, since each consecutive step is taken at a higher level than the previous one, part of the descending parabola is 'cut' during the air phase. Therefore, injuries to the hamstring (as well as the traumas due to the impact of the body to the ground) are less likely to appear than in sprinting on level ground.

Furthermore, I would like to underline that the component of explosiveness recovery is much more important in 80 to 100 meter running repetitions on level ground (specifically after the first 25 to 30 meters) than in uphill running. I also want to point out that it is still more significant than in acceleration running phases, which are much more frequent than spurting phases during the course of a soccer match.

Uphill repetitions and strength

Uphill running also strengthens lower limb muscles more than running on level ground. As far as this physical attribute is concerned, it is proven that it decreases less than in lactic acid exercise on level ground. Greater forces must be exerted by the body to move uphill and this obviously involves a considerable number of fast-conducting fibers which are therefore highly stimulated during exercise. Since physical effort is gradually protracted over increasingly long periods of time, fast-conducting fibers can progressively enhance their endurance levels, in the sense that they can gradually remove the lactic acid they have manufactured much more rapidly, or even absorb it and maybe use larger amounts of oxygen.

Uphill repetitions and 'Fascetti's effect'

Attention should also be focused on quickness, another subject of crucial importance which I refer to as 'Fascetti's effect'. When I was the fitness coach of Varese soccer club in the Italian Serie B, Coach Eugenio Fascetti realized that one single training session mainly based on uphill running usually sufficed to help his players recover their original efficiency in case of lackluster performances. I cannot explain why this happened, but all the observations directly made 'on the field' cannot be fully explained in a rational way.

Nevertheless, this does not mean they must be totally rejected.

That important observation - which I could also verify on other occasions during my personal career - clearly helped me to realize that including uphill running repetitions in the pre-season training plan also allowed my players to enhance their sprinting skills so that they could play pre-season matches in much better physical conditions (they usually outran their opponents in sprints). When I would suggest lactic acid exercise on level ground including 150 to 300 meter repetitions in the past, my players were generally unable to change their pace, sprint and move their lower limbs very quickly. Although that physical exercise was much harder and uphill repetitions more demanding (both at muscular and organic level) than running repetitions on level ground, my players could always be quite quick.

Uphill repetitions and endurance

When a player performs twenty uphill repetitions or more of 60 or 70 meters each (see the conditioning progression in paragraph 7.2) in one single training session and also repeats the same exercise some times within a few days, not only does he train his central aerobic components and all the mechanisms responsible for promptly removing lactic acid, but he also enhances several other components of endurance, like those connected to the psychological aspect, those influenced by the temperature-water-salt balance and those which directly depend on glycogen stores. In this sense, uphill lactic acid exercise can help players enhance their endurance skills so as to successfully endure the 90 minutes of a soccer match.

Uphill repetitions and running skills in soccer

Some people still believe that soccer players can really benefit from nothing but the situations approaching real-game conditions. It is still difficult for some coaches to believe that a certain kind of exercise - a specific kind or running, in particular - can be highly beneficial not because it reproduces real soccer situations, but because it brings about important changes in the body.

In particular, uphill running plays a role of critical importance since it allows athletes to practice at much higher power levels than in physical exercise on level ground. This causes a more rapid increase in the heart rate (which is specifically useful to enhance central aerobic components) on one hand, and sensible lactic acid production on the other.

Moreover, uphill running is fundamental since it involves specific mechanical forces and muscular work which paradoxically approach acceleration mechanisms (which are highly specific to soccer players) much more than other kinds or running which quickly raise the heart rate and stimulate the production of considerable amounts of lactic acid - like 100 to 150 meter (or more) repetitions, for instance.

Different uphill conditioning methods

In order to conclude what I have told you about my personal uphill training methods up to now, I think it is also advisable to describe how other fitness coaches plan uphill running.

Uphill running repetitions according to Prof. Pincolini

Prof. Vincenzo Pincolin divides uphill running repetitions into three groups:
- long uphill repetitions: up to nearly 80 meters;
- middle uphill repetitions: up to nearly 40 meters;
- short uphill repetitions: up to nearly 15 meters.

Pincolini's pre-season conditioning plan includes uphill running twice to 3 times a week, with a two-day interval between two consecutive sessions of this kind, for a total of 10 training sessions in about one month. Over this period of time, he suggests up to 20 long and middle repetitions (in the same session, too), which could be planned as follows:
- 2 sets of 5 40 meter uphill running repetitions with a recovery interval of about 40 seconds between two consecutive repetitions and a pause of 1 min. 30 sec to 2 minutes between the first and the second set;
- 2 sets of 3 60 meter uphill repetitions with a recovery interval of about 60 minutes between two consecutive repetitions and a pause of 2 minutes to 2 min 30 sec between the first and the second set;
- 4 uphill running repetitions of 80 meters each with a recovery interval of about 1 min 30 sec between two consecutive repetitions.

On the other hand, during the course of the soccer season Prof. Pincolini prefers to use various uphill running in a much more specific manner: in other words, he chooses specific uphill running repetitions in direct relation to the physical skills he intends to train. So, during the conditioning macro-cycle he typically suggests (for the mid-week training session - on Wednesday in general):

- long uphill running repetitions (up to 80 meters) in the training week specifically focused on lactic acid exercise; his conditioning plan includes 2 sets of 4 80 meter uphill repetitions with a recovery interval of about 1 min 30 sec between two consecutive repetitions, and a pause of 3 minutes between the first and the second set;
- middle uphill running repetitions (up to 40 meters) in the training week based on non lactic acid exercise; for instance: 2 sets of 5 uphill repetitions with a recovery interval of about 40 to 45 seconds between two consecutive repetitions and 2 minutes between the two sets;
- short uphill running repetitions (up to 15 meters) every week, including the week specifically dedicated to warm down light exercise; he firmly believes that these short repetitions are particularly helpful for players to enhance their sprinting skills and quickness.

Uphill running repetitions according to Prof. Sassi

Roberto Sassi's conditioning plans also include extra long uphill repetitions - lasting about 3 minutes - in addition to short (15 meters), middle (30 meters) and long (70 to 100 meters) running repetitions.

Over the pre-season training period, he suggests:

- uphill running over distances of about 90 meters in a natural environment, starting from 6 repetitions (2 sets of 3 repetitions each) up to 20 (4 sets of 5 repetitions); the recovery interval between two consecutive repetitions fall from 2 min. in the first session to 1 min 30 sec in the last one, while the pause between the various sets drops from 4 to 3 minutes; the coach should avoid suggesting these uphill repetitions for two days before running;
- extra long uphill repetitions (of about 3 minutes), with recovery intervals of about 5 to 6 minutes; 6 to 8 repetitions at most, for a total of 3 or 4 training sessions over the pre-season conditioning period (this kind of uphill running should be avoided during the soccer season).

Sassi's training master plan during the season includes uphill running in mid-week; it also combines different uphill repetitions (15 at least), starting from long-distance exercise and gradually shifting to

shorter repetitions as follows:
• 5 x 100 meters + 5 x 50 meters + 5 x 30 meters
or
• 10 x 50 meters + 5 x 30 meters.

Sassi sometimes combines 25 meter uphill running repetitions with running on level ground (a few meters) between two consecutive repetitions. The recovery interval between two consecutive repetitions is always 1 minute to 1 min. 30 sec, while the pause between the sets is 2 to 3 minutes, in general.

Uphill running repetitions according to Prof. Asnaghi

Prof. Gigi Asnaghi suggests uphill running repetitions over various distances (long, middle and short distances), but his conditioning master plans also include some other kinds of running exercises which are usually carried out in the mid-week training sessions during the course of the soccer season:
• uphill slalom running; in practice, this exercise reproduces the same pattern of slalom running on level ground; 5 or 6 cones are set from the foot to the peak of the slope; they stand 3 meters apart and each cone is at a distance of about 1 meter to the side compared to the previous one. Compared to the same exercise on level ground, uphill slalom running involves much more sensible deceleration while running around the cones and acceleration obviously requires greater physical effort;
• 'fast and loose' uphill runs to alternate sprinting repetitions (10 to 30 meters) at full speed with running (10 meters or even less, in general); the distance the athlete covers at full speed should not exceed 60 meters.

7.5 Uphill running repetitions during the soccer season and possible alternative solutions

I have already pointed out that 60 to 70 meter uphill running repetitions are certainly very demanding at both the muscular and organic level. This is why I usually prefer to avoid using them during the course of the season. I am still convinced that players cannot completely recover from the fatigue deriving from long uphill running before the match, but my fears could probably prove groundless in the next few years, when athletes will be trained better than today and will be able to recover from such physical stresses. There are some alternative training methods whose final effects are very similar to uphill running since they also bring about a rapid increase in the heart rate and therefore enhance central aerobic components. First of all, these alternative solutions include all the training methods suggested for the lactic acid mechanism, which will be clearly referred to in chapter eight, they also cause the heart rate to rise quickly. Some particular Fartlek exercises - those which involve a stimulus of short duration, but very sudden changes of pace - can also be highly effective. In this context, I also include the training method suggested by Prof. Bosco, that is running with changes of pace. High intensity physical exercise with the ball could also be a very effective solution. I think that coaches should also focus their attention on these important alternative solutions while planning pre-season training.

Lactic Acid
Energy Components

Today, some fitness coaches still believe that the lactic acid components of endurance, namely, all those energy components which are directly connected to lactic acid production in muscles, are not particularly important in soccer, and, therefore, soccer players do not need to train them specifically. On the contrary, I firmly believe that not only do soccer players' muscles produce considerable amounts of lactate during the course of a match, but it is fundamental for them to regularly train their lactic acid energy mechanisms - all those components which are specific to this physical activity.

Lactic acid production in soccer

Many different factors allow us to state with absolute certainty that the lactic acid mechanism plays a role of critical importance in soccer. First of all, there are several theoretical assumptions. On one side lactic acid production is very likely to occur during one single effort of a few seconds (see paragraph 8.1.1). On the other hand, the lactic acid mechanism can also be activated when very short physical efforts - whose single duration would not bring about lactate production - are carried out within a very short time (see paragraph 8.1.2). Both situations may occur - or, better: regularly occur - in soccer. Careful research carried out on blood samples taken from soccer players playing at different levels during and after the match, always prove considerable concentrations of such metabolite, especially in higher-level players (see paragraph 8.1.3).

Lactate production during
very short physical activity

Professors Margaria, Cerretelli and Mangili discovered that maximal intensity physical activity which promptly led the athlete to total exhaustion within 5 seconds (for instance, running at a speed of 18 kilometers an hour on a hill with a gradient of 1 in 4) considerably rose blood lactate concentration, which proved to be twice as much as the standard concentration in an individual at rest (see diagram 8.1). In such situations, the lactic acid mechanism significantly contributes to the production of energy: its contribution to energy release accounts for about 42%.

Common workouts of very short duration (5 seconds, for example) causing upper limbs to work at maximal intensity, also bring about a remarkable increase in blood lactate concentration, which proves to be nearly 4 times higher than standard values.

Diagram 8.1 shows that the lactic acid mechanism is also involved in physical activities whose duration is shorter than 5 seconds - even 2 seconds, in some cases. This is possible during special muscular workouts requiring (and releasing) great power from the very beginning of the exercise. In other words, a 25 to 30 yards sprint at maximal intensity is likely to stimulate significant lactate production, especially in those athletes whose muscles are particularly rich in fast-conducting fibers favoring sudden and violent spurts.

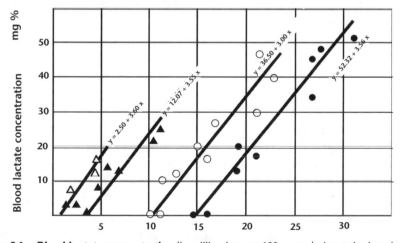

Diagram 8.1 - Blood lactate concentration (in millimoles per 100 grams) above the basal level, in sedentary people who ran at a speed of 18 km/h on hills with different slopes: a 25%, 20%, 15% and 10% gradient respectively. The four lines - from the left to the right - show the four different slopes. The peak of the line refers to the 'exhaustion time', which is a little more than 5 seconds in the case of highest-intensity exercise (the left line). The several points in the middle refer to the values of blood lactate concentration when the analyzed individuals did not get to exhaustion. By carefully observing that line, we can clearly understand that lactic acid begins to be produced above standard levels in the blood after 2 seconds.

8.1.2 Lactate production resulting from consecutive efforts carried out within a very short time

It is proven that the sole non lactic acid energy mechanism is activated in most muscular activities in soccer when several seconds (or even a few minutes) elapse between two consecutive physical efforts and that mechanism exploits those energy sources (ATP stored in muscle tissue and CP, or phosphocreatine in particular) which do not bring about lactate production - as explained in chapter four.

In real-game situations, the soccer player is often forced to make several consecutive efforts within a very short time, when part of the total CP has not been newly synthesized, (when his 'non lactic acid oxygen debt' has not been replaced). Non lactic acid oxygen can usually be replaced rather quickly. This situation promptly results in the activation of the lactic acid energy mechanism: this means that muscle tissue manufactures a certain amount of lactic acid which subsequently enters the blood stream.

8.1.3 Lactate concentrations after the first half of the match and at the end of the competition

Several researchers have measured blood lactate concentrations in soccer players. For instance, in 1981 Ekblom and his team measured blood lactate concentrations in athletes playing in different leagues at the end of the first half of the match and after the competition. As you can clearly see in diagram 8.2, the higher the level of the team, the higher the values on average.

In the same way, blood lactate values are higher after the first 45 minutes than at the end of the match. Remember that the decrease in blood lactate concentration at the end of the competition compared to the values after the first half is very likely to be due to the gradual depletion of muscle glycogen stores as the end of the match approaches (for further details see diagram 8.3.)

The maximal values of lactate concentration measured in soccer players (diagram 8.2) are certainly lower (nearly 50% lower) than those measured in top-level 400, 800 or 1,500 meter runners immediately after a race. Nevertheless, it would be completely wrong to believe that the lactic acid mechanism plays a role of minor importance in soccer. The average height of soccer players is lower than top-class high jumpers, but this does not mean that height is not important in soccer. The soccer player needs a wide range of

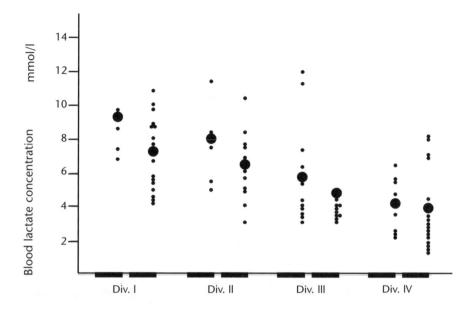

Diagram 8.2 - Soccer players' **blood lactate concentrations** in millimoles per liter. 'Div. I' refers to the highest level and corresponds to the Italian Serie A. While moving to the right of the abscissa, the soccer levels get increasingly lower. For each level, the diagram shows both the lactate concentrations after the first half (on the left), and the values at the end of the match (on the right). As you can see, blood lactate concentrations at the end of the competition are lower than those at the end of the first half, on the average; in the same way, the lower the level, the lower all the average values (bigger black circles).

attributes and skills and it is inconceivable that he should and could reach maximum values for each one of them, in the same way as the athletes for whom that particular attribute or quality is typically fundamental for their particular disciplines and performances.

As far as the lactic acid components of endurance are concerned, it is important to underline that high lactate concentrations and high acidity values - like those which are very likely to be measured in 400, 800 and 1,500 meter runners - considerably influence the full efficiency of the central nervous system. While this condition could be compatible with an cyclical physical activity like running it would be totally incompatible with an acyclic activity such as soccer. The performance would be negatively affected since quick reflexes, coordination and mental lucidity would be obviously impaired in such difficult conditions.

In short, if we consider all the information and data we have at our disposal, there is no doubt that soccer players apply to the lactic acid anaerobic energy mechanism during the course of a soccer match.

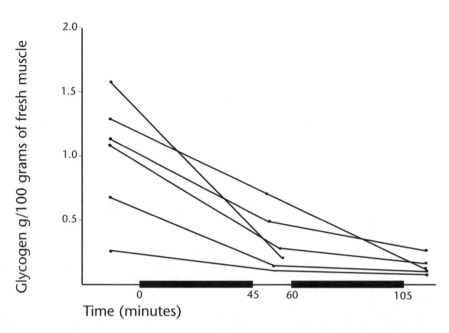

Diagram 8.3 - Glycogen concentration in the vastus lateralis muscle, in grams per 100 grams of fresh muscle, in soccer players playing in the Swedish first division championship. Glycogen concentration was measured before the match, at half time and at the end of the competition; glycogen was almost totally used up by the end of the match.

Physiology of the lactic acid energy mechanism

At the end of chapter three we explained that endurance in soccer can be defined as the ability to maintain the performance (from the technical, tactical, athletic... points of view) at constant levels over an extended period of time, in spite of the great amount of physical exercise carried out. In this sense, the lactic acid energy mechanism also plays a role of crucial importance.

Understanding how the lactic acid energy mechanism really works is fundamental to understanding all those special conditioning methods which definitely enhance the lactic acid components of endurance. Only through a deep knowledge of the subject is it possible to understand how special training can bring about the desired changes and adjustments in the athlete's body.

Lactic acid production and removal

Lactic acid is manufactured in muscle fibers, or better in the cytoplasm. It is mainly produced from glucose molecules which split off from glycogen stored in those muscle fibers. In reality, in the cytoplasm lactic acid is almost totally (1,249 molecules out of 1,250) dissociated into lactate ion - with a negative charge (LA-) - and hydrogen ion - with a positive charge (H+). From the muscle fibers where it is first produced lactic acid spreads into extracellular fluids; the LA- molecule moves out much more slowly than the H+ molecule - which is considerably smaller - and can then penetrate either into blood capillaries or into other close muscle fibers (see 8.4).

Lactate can be manufactured in a fast-conducting fiber, flow out of it and spread into a slow-conducting fiber, where it is synthesized into pyruvate molecules, carried into the mitochondria and finally used as 'fuel' to release energy. The LA- molecules flowing into the blood stream bring about a sudden variation in lactacidemia (that is blood lactate concentration). Such a variation can be easily measured through blood sampling. While the blood of an individual who has been at rest for several hours contains about 1 millimole of lactic acid per liter (and his muscle tissue contains 1 millimole per kilogram of muscle), blood lactate concentration values are considerably higher both during and after a soccer match - as was shown in diagram 8.1.

However, LA- molecules are eventually removed from the blood. Some special organs (the heart, the liver, the kidneys and, above all, some muscles other than those which previously produced them) 'suck them up' from the blood stream and either directly use them as fuel to release energy or synthesize them into glycogen.

Physical disorders brought about by lactate and hydrogen ions

When lactic acid concentration exceeds certain levels in muscle fibers, it inhibits the activity of some important enzymes, such as phosphorylase, phosphofructokinase and lactate dehydrogenase. This obviously impairs the efficiency of the muscle. Hydrogen ions tend to raise the acidity in the fiber itself. Fortunately, the cytoplasm also contains special buffer solutions - most of them proteins - which help to mitigate their negative effects. An increase in the acidity of muscle fibers is very likely to cause a decrease in the force those fibers can exert and, therefore, 'knock them out' for a certain period of time - the time necessary to restore the starting conditions. When hydrogen ions (H+) flow into extracellular fluids and then into the blood, they promptly find other special buffers - the bicarbonates, in particular. As previously stated, the increase in muscle fiber

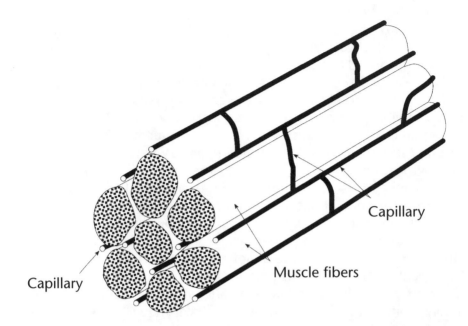

Diagram 8.4 - This diagram shows the arrangement of both capillaries and muscle fibers within the muscle; we can imagine that lactic acid is produced in some of these fibers (for instance, in those with larger cross sections, like that at the top of the drawing or that just below it on the left; these can be considered as fast-conducting fibers). Lactate ions partly flow out of the fibers where they were produced and spread into extracellular fluids; in this way, they can penetrate the capillaries and therefore enter the blood stream in order to cir-culate through the whole body. Blood sampling allows you to discover an increase in lactate concentration after a physical effort which obviously brought about an increase in lactic acid production. However, lactate ions can flow from extracellular fluids into muscle fibers close to the fibers where they were previously produced; in these fibers, they can be syn-thesized into pyruvate ions and finally carried into the mitochondria to be used by the aero-bic energy mechanism.

acidity which may occur can seriously damage the central nervous system, thus impairing muscular coordination, the accuracy of one's movements, quick reflexes and so forth.

Considering these serious negative effects on the central nervous system (in addition to the negative consequences on muscles effi-ciency), there is no doubt that high lactate and H+ concentrations do not allow soccer players to endure fatigue and maintain their athletic, technical and tactical levels for an extended period of time.

Lactic acid's travel through the body

We could schematically imagine that, once lactic acid has been produced in muscle fibers, it can be found in three different places: in the muscles where it was previously manufactured; in the blood; or in the organs which are responsible for gradually removing it. It takes a certain time for lactic acid to flow from one place to another.

For instance, it takes some minutes for a perfect balance between the muscle fiber and the blood to be possible, even though the release of lactic acid from the fiber itself is favored by a special carrier (that is a molecule which helps to transport it outside). For example, if an individual ran 300 or 400 meters at top intensity, his blood lactate concentrations would rise only 4 to 8 minutes later.

The process by which lactate is completely removed from the blood follows a special development which could be described by referring to the so-called 'half-replacement period'. For example, the 'half-replacement period' of a sedentary person is about 15 minutes. This means that if blood lactate concentration rises to maximum levels (let's suppose 8 millimoles/liter) 4 to 8 minutes after exercise, the value will be reduced by a half (that is 4 millimoles/liter) 15 minutes later. Another 15 minutes later, blood lactic acid concentration will be reduced by another half (2 mmol/l) and 45 minutes after exercise it will be restored to standard levels (1 mmol/l). In well-trained athletes, the above-mentioned 'half-replacement period' is obviously lower, even below 6 to 7 minutes in some cases. This means that it takes an 18 to 21 minutes interval (or even less) for their blood lactate concentrations to drop from as much as 8 mmol/l to basal levels.

Considering the orders of size of the lactic acid's movements from one place to another, it is obvious that:

- the lactic acid stored in muscles plays a very important role in those competitions whose duration does not exceed several seconds (400 meters in running and 100 meters in swimming, for instance). Very little lactate can flow into the blood stream within a very short time.
- the blood is also important in competitions lasting several minutes (like 3,000 meter running or swimming 800 meters (women) and 1,500 meters (men). While the athlete is still performing physical activity, part of the lactic acid present in muscles can leave muscle fibers, flow into extracellular fluids and therefore penetrate into the capillaries;

- in soccer, where the performance is carried out for extended periods of time and involving lactic acid production, not only can lactate enter the blood stream, but it is also removed from the blood - in part, at least - by the several organs which are responsible for this special activity.

A hydraulic model reproducing the lactic acid energy mechanism

To understand some important features of the lactic acid energy mechanism let's look at a special hydraulic model, like that in diagram 8.5. This model consists of 9 basins: the basin in the upper part of the structure represents a glycogen reservoir. This basin is connected to a faucet which then divides into two separate pipes: one for H+ ions, the other for LA- ions. Hydrogen ions (H+) flow into basin F (that is into muscle fibers), but a considerable amount of them can easily slip (the connecting tube is quite large) into basin B1, corresponding to the buffers present in the fiber itself - these buffers are mostly proteins. Another quantity of H+ leave the muscle fiber and spread into extracellular fluids (basin EF); in this situation, there is a loss of H+ ions (suggested by the exhaust device) which stands for the total amount of hydrogen ions buffered by the bicarbonates occurring in extracellular fluids.

A large amount of H+ ions enter the blood stream (basin BS) and part of them flow out into basin B2, corresponding to blood buffers - bicarbonates, in particular. Some of those hydrogen ions are also likely to be removed from the blood - in the hydraulic model shown in diagram 8.5 this is possible through the exhaust device.

If there are five basins for H+ ions on one side, on the other there are just three for lactate ions, since the two basins corresponding to the buffering activity in muscle fibers and in the blood do not exist. However, lactate ions also move from the cytoplasm of the muscle fibers where they were produced (basin F) to extracellular fluids (basin EF). Here, there is little loss of LA- ions (through the small exhaust device): these ions penetrate into close muscle fibers, which finally use them. A larger amount of LA- ions contained in extracellular fluids flow into the blood, from which they are finally removed (exhaust device).

This hydraulic model can help to understand: the travels of H+ and LA- ions from one section to another; the buffering activity against H+ ions (both in muscle fibers and in the blood); the role of muscle glycogen depletion and so forth. Obviously, this is a very

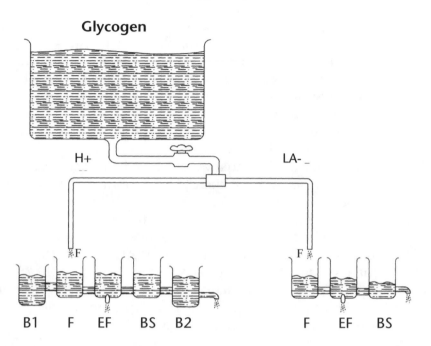

Diagram 8.5 - Hydraulic model reproducing the lactic acid energy mechanism.

simplified model. Only one muscle fiber is represented instead of the thousands of fibers which simultaneously produce H+ and LA- ions in every muscle. There is no correct proportion of the capacities of the several basins since the volume of those muscles where LA- and H+ ions are supposed to be produced during the course of a soccer match is 2.5 times as much as the volume of the blood and four times as much as the volume of extracellular fluids. Also, it does not consider the fact that the flow of ions from one section to another is much more complex than the movement from one basin to the other through a simple tube. Nevertheless, we hope that it will help to better understand how the lactic acid energy mechanism works in practice.

Special features of the lactic acid components of endurance in soccer

The explanations given in the previous paragraphs help us understand that the lactic acid energy mechanism is rather complex. Perhaps, those who deny the importance of this mechanism in soccer do not really know its physiological features.

When referring to the definition of 'endurance' given at the beginning of paragraph 8.2 - which lays particular emphasis on the importance of maintaining the performance at constant levels in spite of the considerable volume of physical work carried out - I would say that, for soccer players to maintain their maximal efficiency, their physical capacities play a crucial role and should be properly trained in order to:

- remove the lactic acid produced in muscles by means of a suitable metabolic process;
- fight and lessen the negative effects of hydrogen ions.

In general, when speaking of energy mechanisms, we refer to the basic concepts of 'power' and 'capacity' of such processes. In the specific case of the lactic acid mechanism, the word 'power' refers to the total amount of lactic acid ATP produced in the unit of time, while 'capacity' means the total quantity of ATP manufactured by that mechanism during the course of the competition. In short, while referring to soccer in particular, it is possible to underline that:

- Lactic acid power plays an important role when the player performs physical activities at top intensity, that is when he sprints or spurts at the top of his capacities. In these situations, part of the ATP used by his muscles is provided by the lactic acid energy mechanism. The capacity to produce larger amounts of lactic acid ATP per minute (which means a high lactic acid power) clearly provides muscles with more ATP: this consequently means that the player can spurt faster;
- Lactic acid capacity does not refer only to the player's muscle lactate concentration at the end of the match or at half time; nor does it refer only to the total amount of lactate stored in muscles and in the blood (which is the case of activities and competitions lasting some minutes, like 3,000-meter running in track and field). Rather, lactic acid capacity in soccer also considers the amount of lactic acid removed during the course of the match; as to hydrogen ions, not only is it fundamental to consider those which are still stored in muscles, but also the ions which previously flowed into the blood and those whose negative effects have been gradually neutralized as well.

Training the Lactic Acid Components of Endurance

Many times we have pointed out that the lactic acid energy mechanism is activated during the course of a match and that it results in the formation of 'waste products' (H+ ions and lactate ions) which directly upset both physical and mental efficiency. 'Waste products' formation is not constant and depends on the special kind of muscular work carried out during the match and on the physical qualities of every single player. Consequently, the production of both hydrogen and lactate ions can significantly vary from one player to another. A large amount of H+ and LA- ions are removed during the course of the competition. The loss of these ions can be further enhanced and made much quicker by means of specific training. The total amounts of lactic acid ATP produced during exercise being equal, special conditioning methods can help to reduce undesired negative effects in the athlete. Also, physical disorders being equal, they can help to produce and provide muscles with larger quantities of ATP. In my opinion, this is particularly important in relation to what endurance really means in soccer, that is the capacity to maintain the performance - athletic, tactical, technical and so forth - at constant levels even after strenuous physical exercise.

Physical adjustments brought about by special training

In the last paragraph of chapter eight, we discussed the meaning of 'lactic acid capacity' in soccer. This important capacity can be further enhanced by means of exercise and special training. Theoretically, as far as hydrogen ions are concerned, specific exercise is supposed to bring about the following adjustments in the athlete's body:

• the buffering capacity in muscle fibers can be considerably enhanced, especially because of the increased production of carnosine and other dipeptides and tripeptides (in the hydraulic model of the lactic acid mechanism shown in diagram 8.5 on page 74, this situation would cause basin B1 to become larger);

- in the same way, the buffering capacity in extracellular fluids can be significantly intensified (as if basin EF in diagram 8.5 became larger) and the flowing of hydrogen ions into other fibers is boosted (as if the exhaust device in basin EF had a larger diameter);
- the buffering capacity and the capacity to remove H+ ions can be considerably stimulated in the blood (as if basin B2 and the diameter of its exhaust device became larger).

As to lactate ions (LA-), the physical changes resulting from specific training could be schematically summarized as follows:

- the passage from muscle fibers to extracellular fluids becomes much quicker (the diameter of the tube linking basin F to basin EF becomes larger);
- more lactic acid penetrates into close muscle fibers, which promptly metabolize it (the diameter of the exhaust device in basin EF becomes larger);
- the amount of lactate which is removed from the blood in the unit of time significantly rises (the diameter of the exhaust device in basin BS becomes larger).

It is important to remember that lactate metabolization directly brings about a decrease in acidity levels. In practice, it is as if one hydrogen ion (H+) disappeared - through a process opposite to the mechanism leading to lactate formation - per every molecule of lactic acid which is completely 'burnt' to carbon dioxide and water (or synthesized to glucose).

Special exercise is also supposed to raise muscle glycogen concentration and this effect should be considered particularly important. The increase in muscle glycogen concentration is very likely to result from the fact that the athlete gradually gets accustomed to performing such physical activities which cause lactic acid to be produced in large amounts and therefore help the depletion of muscle glycogen stores.

9.2 The best methods for training the lactic acid components of endurance in a highly specific manner

I suggest planning special training to include some particular moments of lactic acid formation, in very large amounts and at suitable intervals of several minutes. For professional players who are accustomed to this kind of work, I suggest 5 to 7 lactic acid periods, at intervals of about 12 minutes at the beginning. The recovery intervals can be gradually reduced to 8 minutes or even less if this kind of work is regularly carried out in the week training cycle. In much simpler words, this exercise is aimed at stimulating the body to produce sufficient amounts of lactic acid 5 to 7 times, so as to gradually get used to enduring and removing it more and more quickly; the several components of lactic acid endurance are trained in the intervals between two consecutive periods of lactic acid exercise.

In practice, the most specific training methods for enhancing lactate production can be classified as follows:

• 1 - One single running repetition lasting several seconds: from 15-20 to 45-50 seconds when running on level ground, and even less when training on hills. The athletes run at a speed close to the maximum speed at which they would be able to run that repetition. In particular, this group includes:

    • linear running track (that is on a track which does not force the athlete to slow down and change direction or turn around) over distances of about 150 to 300 meters, in general;

    • 'shuttle' running ('go and run back') over typical distances of about 25 to 50 meters; the athlete runs up and back repeatedly until he covers the desired distance (for instance, he can cover a distance of 200 meters by running up and back 4 times over 50 meters);

    • hill running track, 60-70 to 100 meters long.

• 2 - Repetitions performed over short distances, at top speed and with an interval of a few seconds between two consecutive repetitions (only in some particular cases are recovery intervals close to 30 seconds); no physical activity is carried out during recovery intervals - only jogging should be allowed. These running repetitions can last from 3 seconds (which correspond to about 20 meters on level ground) to 6-7 seconds at most; apart from typical forward running and spurts, these repetitions can also include other kinds of running exercise (backward and sideways running, sideways sliding, hurdling, etc...) as well as decelerations, changes of direction and turn around in many different possible combinations. As it will be explained below, the recovery interval should not be excessively long in order to avoid favoring the complete re-synthesis of phosphocreatine. In particular, this group of repetitions includes the following conditioning methods:

- accelerations on level ground performed over rather short distances (15-20 to 40-50 meters in general), and repeated either a few or several times with a short recovery interval between two consecutive accelerations;
- 'sprint and release' running exercise on level ground, with an overall duration of about 10-15 to 25-30 seconds: It combines high-intensity activity with 'recovery periods' involving less strenuous exercise. A typical example of this kind of work is a 200 meter run: every 20 meters, the athlete alternates between sprinting and jogging;
- sprints on hills performed over distances of about 30 to 50-60 meters, repeated a few or several times.

While carrying out the activities belonging to the first group, lactic acid is produced in considerable amounts, because every single exercise requires the significant intervention of the anaerobic lactic acid mechanism by itself.

As to the activities included in the second group, each exercise - considered separately from the others - would cause the production of very small amounts of lactic acid or even no lactate formation at all. However, since every consecutive sprint is performed within a very short time from the previous one - that is when the athlete has not been able to replace his non lactic acid oxygen debt (which means that there has not been enough time for him to re-synthesize all the phosphocreatine he has used up, but only a very small amount in some cases) - the most favorable conditions occur for lactic acid to be produced in increasingly large amounts during each consecutive exercise. 'Lactic acid power' plays a crucial role in the physical activities of this second group and not only does this have significant training effects on such qualities as quickness, agility, lucidity and so forth, but on lactic acid power itself.

I think that a conditioning session specifically designed for training the lactic acid energy mechanism should include at least 5 different lactic acid exercises of either the first or the second type with a recovery interval of several minutes between two consecutive activities. In general, I prefer to begin the training session by suggesting longer and low-intensity workouts (those belonging to group 1.1 or group 1.2, for instance). More demanding muscular exercises (those of the second group) are typically performed in the central part of the session, while I sometimes plan other low-intensity activities (of type 1.1 or 1.2) at the end of the session. As far as the recovery periods are concerned, I suggest different workouts which do not require large energy expense, but stimulate great concentration and/or muscular explosiveness, like skips, hops, slaloms, hurdling and so forth.

Soccer players' difficulties when taking lactic acid exercise

When using other conditioning methods, it is much easier for coaches to plan and check the work carried out by directly referring to standard accurate and personalized parameters. When referring to aerobic peripheral components of endurance, for instance, the coach can previously set - by small margin of errors - the best running pace for each player whose features and abilities he knows well. Furthermore, he can also assess whether the player has been training hard and effectively or not by accurately timing his performance.

On the contrary, this is much more difficult when referring to lactic acid exercise. In some particular cases, it would be possible to check the real work carried out, for instance when players run 150 or 200 meters (but remember that the distance must be measured very accurately!), or 20 meters + 20 meters 'shuttle' running repetitions, or 60 meter long hill repetitions. Nevertheless, in most cases coaches will have serious difficulties assessing and measuring training carried out, both because a coach usually works with about twenty players at a time and because it is almost impossible to accurately check real total or partial distances covered by the athletes - especially when running activities also include changes of directions and combinations of running exercises. On the other hand, I believe that the coach should avoid always suggesting the same kinds of exercise when planning a lactic acid training session, simply because they help him to measure and quantify his players' performances. I firmly believe that the coach should be creative and constantly vary the activities, while always choosing among those which stimulate large lactate production.

Psychological factors also play a crucial role in lactic acid conditioning exercise. The athlete should always perform these activities with the greatest concentration and at top intensity so as to enhance lactic acid formation, and the fitness coach and/or the coach should know both the general effects of this kind of work and the direct effects on every single player. He should always be ready to stimulate and encourage those who do not train properly and at the suitable intensity to favor lactate production, which is the final purpose of this kind of exercise.

Unlike middle and long distance runners, soccer players usually accept lactic acid activities much more willingly than the workouts especially designed for peripheral aerobic components like 800 or 1,000 meter running repetitions. I do not think it is worthwhile planning more than one lactic acid training session a week during the season. I am convinced that - unlike what typically occurs with specific aerobic conditioning (where the player's performance is very likely to benefit from an increased number of special training sessions) - practicing more than once a week is not really helpful in this particular case. However, I am ready to change my mind if, in the future, it is proven that more special conditioning exercise is required for players to further enhance their capacities to endure fatigue.

Table 9.1
In this table, I will describe some of the special conditioning methods used for training the lactic acid components of endurance.

'Shuttle' running exercise over distances of 100 to 300 meters. Players perform 100 to 200 meter (and up to 300 meter, in some cases) 'shuttle' running repetitions, which means that they run there and back along the same basic track, which is usually 25, 33 or 50 meters long. This method for running lactic acid repetitions was designed by Massimo Begnis, who made a virtue of necessity - as they say - since he had no suitable large spaces for training his athletes. In practice, players run along the same set track for a certain number of times, until they cover the desired distance; obviously, at the end of the track, they must quickly stop, turn around and change direction. For instance, in the case of 100 meter 'shuttle' running exercise, players run either four times (twice there and twice back) along a 25 meter long track, or three times (twice there and 1 back) along a track 33 meters long. Every player should cover such a distance at an intensity close to the maximal intensity at which he would be able to cover it.

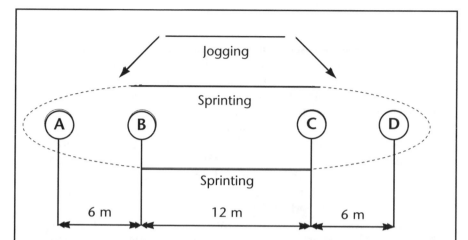

Diagram 9.1 - 'Sprint and release' exercise. Position four cones so as to mark out a circuit: the first and the second cone are 4 to 8 meters apart - exactly like the third and the fourth; while the distance between the second and the third is double. Players run in an Indian line, 2 or 3 meters apart; for instance, they run 4 laps moving around the cones, alternating at top speed (straight line in the diagram) with jogging (sketched line).

'Sprint and release' exercise. This special activity combines jogging and sprints at peak intensity. For instance, it is possible to divide the length of the playing field into 8 different segments of 12 meters each; players will cover the whole length of the field alternating jogging and sprinting segments. So if they need to cover a distance of 200 meters, they will run the long side of the field there and back. The coach can freely vary the length of the segments into which the playing field is divided; in general, it is from 8 to 20 meters. However, this kind of exercise can also be performed in a special running circuit, like that shown in diagram 9.1, whose overall perimeter is 48 meters (but it can be either shorter or longer, according to the needs). In this situation, the players position a couple of meters apart in Indian file, jog along one length of the circuit and sprint at top intensity along the following one. The same circuit can be covered several times, usually twice to four times. For instance, the players can run four laps: which means an overall distance of about 200 meters, half of which are sprints.

Repeated sprints. Players run at top speed over distances of 20 to 60 meters. This kind of work can be carried out in different manners: for instance, the distance that players will cover can either remain unchanged, for instance 40 meters or alternate 20 meters with 30, 40 and 50 meters in the same set of repetitions. During the recovery period in every set of sprints, the players can be completely at rest or jog so as to cover the same distance previously covered while sprinting (since this special work to train the lactic acid components of endurance, remember that the recovery interval should always be very short - in general, no more than a few seconds). The recovery time will be longer between two consecutive sets of sprints.

Run there and back. Like in 'shuttle' running exercise, players run there and back several times along the same set track; however, in this case the basic tracks are much shorter (only rarely are they longer than 12 meters) and athletes run at top speed. One of these special running exercises is schematically shown in diagram 9.2, in which a 5 meter long there-and-back runs alternate with a 10 meter long there-and-back run, for a total distance of 60 meters and 4 runs there and 4 runs back. Apart from standard forward running, some parts of the circuit can also include backward or sideways running.

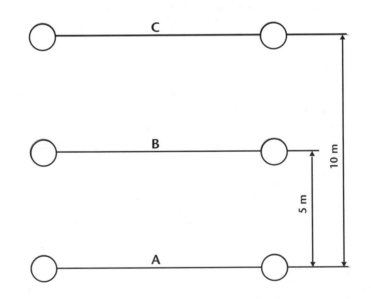

Diagram 9.2 - 'Run there and back' exercise. Players start from line A, run to line B (which are 4 to 8 meters apart), go back to line A; run to line C (which are 8 to 15 meters apart) and move back to line A. Finally they run the same circuits A-B and back, and A-C and back once again.

Hill running repetitions. Obviously, the number of repetitions, the number of sets and the recovery intervals depend on the length of the slope. In addition to the hill running activities previously discussed in chapter seven, I would also like to suggest the so-called 'doublets' and 'triplets'. Since I had no sufficiently long hill tracks, I began to suggest two or three 30 to 40 meter hill running repetitions with no recovery intervals in-between; players were only allowed to jog back to the foot of the slope.

Geometrical figures and letters of the alphabet. In practice, players cover set distances running along non-straight tracks; apart from standard forward running, this exercise also include changes of direction, sudden stops and decelerations, backward and sideways running, sliding and so forth. Coaches and fitness coaches should use their own creativeness to plan new exercises, in relation to the their practical possibilities and their players' needs. Here are some suggestions:

Triangle (diagram 9.3): mark out a 6 by 12 meters equilateral triangle; players can run two or more laps combining different running styles.

Double Z (diagram 9.4): players run along two consecutive Z-shaped tracks and jog to cover the in-between short distance.

Double M (diagram 9.5): in this case, players run along very short tracks (from 3 to 5 meters at most) and suddenly change their directions while also varying their running style.

Diagram 9.3 - 'Triangle' exercise. Forward running along the first side (from A to B in the diagram); backward running along the second side (from B to C) and sideways backward running along the third side of the triangle (from C to A). Once players move back to A, they turn around and change their direction, to run forward from A to C, backward from C to B and sideways from B to A. Obviously, the coach can plan and suggest other combinations and variations of the same exercise.

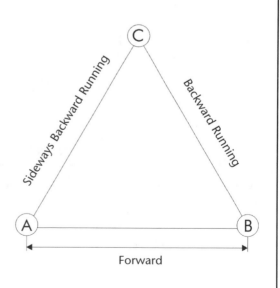

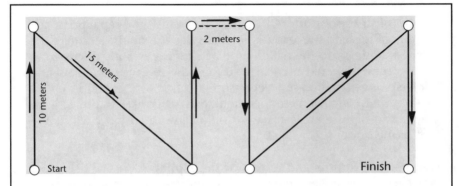

Diagram 9.4 - 'Double Z' exercise. Players run at top speed along two z-shaped tracks and jog to cover the distance between the two tracks. Apart from standard forward running, other running styles are also allowed; for instance, players can alternate forward running with backward running.

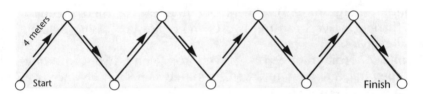

Diagram 9.5 - 'Double M' exercise. This is a typical zig-zag circuit consisting of eight segments which can be covered by alternating standard forward running with other running styles (backward, sideways, sliding and so forth....).

Rhombus (diagram 9.6): two players start simultaneously from each side of a cone; the first 10 meters they run apart, while the following 10 meters they run towards the opposite cone to meet each other. From this position, they turn around and cover the same distance (20 meters) running in the opposite direction.

Star (diagram 9.7): this is very similar to the rhombus exercise, but in this case, two pairs perform the exercise simultaneously in two different rhombi, whose longer diagonals are perpendicular to each other. In practice, it is as if two players started from one corner of a four-end star, and the other two players from the near corner; the running paths of the four players cross each other; consequently, they must pay great attention not to run into each other.

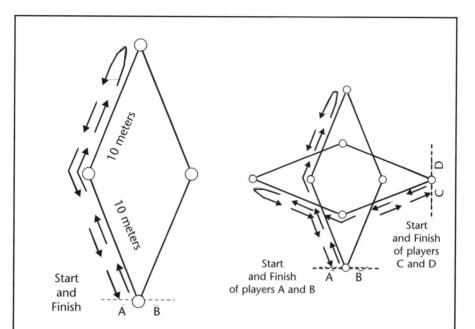

Diagram 9.6 - 'Rhombus' exercise. When the coach or the fitness coach gives the starting signal, two players start from each side of a cone; the first 10 meters they run apart, while the following 10 meters they move towards each other until they reach the opposite cone. From this position, they turn around and run the same 20 meters in the opposite direction.

Diagram 9.7 - 'Star' exercise. In practice, it is exactly like the 'rhombus' exercise, but in this case two pairs perform the exercise simultaneously in two different rhombi crossing each other. Since the paths of the four players meet, they must pay particular attention not to run into each other.

Table 9.2

Here are some examples of lactic acid training plans for athletes who are accustomed to this kind of work. Every training session should begin with proper warm up, including: 10 minutes stretch, 5 minutes to 10 minutes running (or light exercise with the ball), some spurts at increasingly high intensity and a few minutes of skips. The most typically lactic acid activities are especially indicated with an asterisk (*); every training session should include six of them; remember that players should stretch or perform several quickness, agility or explosive power workouts between two consecutive lactic acid exercises. The conditioning plan can also include technical and tactical activities or conditioned games in small spaces.

Example 1 It includes three lactic acid activities of the first group at the beginning: a 300 meter long straight circuit, 250 meters shuttle running exercise and another 200 meters shuttle running; 8 repetitions of 50 meters and two 200 meter 'sprint and release' exercises at the end of the session. This lactic acid work is mostly carried out over longer distances:

- * 1 x 300 m along a straight circuit
- 5 minutes skips
- * 1 x 250 m shuttle running exercise (50 meters long)
- 4 x 5 low hurdling (the hurdles are 1 meter apart), followed by a sprint of 5 meters
- * 1 x 200 m shuttle running exercise (50 meters long)
- 1 x short 'run there and back' (30 meters in total)
- * 2 sets of 4 50 meter running repetitions (recovery intervals: 30 seconds between two
  consecutive repetitions, and 2 minutes between the first and the second set)
- 1 x short 'run there and back' (30 meters in total)
- * 2 sets of 4 'double Z-shaped' running circuits; recovery intervals: 30 seconds between two consecutive repetitions, and 3 minutes between two consecutive sets 5 minutes stretch
- * 2 sets of 'sprint and release' running exercise over a distance of 200 meters (alternate 12.5 m sprinting with 12.5 m running); the recovery period between two consecutive 'sprint and release' activities is 4 minutes.

Example 2 Although this conditioning plan also includes three lactic acid activities of the first group like the first example, it typically suggests much shorter workouts:

- * 1 x 200 meters along a straight circuit
- 4 minutes skips with variations
- * 1 x 150 meter shuttle running exercise (50 meters long)
- hops: four sets of six consecutive hops while running
- * 2 100 meter shuttle running repetitions (50 meters long);
- the recovery intervals between the two exercises is 50 seconds
- 4 sets of 12 meter slalom through the cones
- * 4 sets of (15 m + 25 m + 35 m); running over the same distance the sprint during the recovery interval between two consecutive sprints in each set; the recovery period between two consecutive sets is 1 minute 30 seconds
- 6 10 meter hill running repetitions
- * 2 sets of 100 meter shuttle running repetitions (33 meters long); the recovery period between two consecutive sets is 40 seconds
- 5 minutes stretch

- * 2 sets of 'run there and back' exercise (60 meters in total); 45 seconds recovery between the two sets.

Example 3 It includes two sets of 200 meter repetitions along a straight track followed by several workouts mainly belonging to the second group:
- * 1 x 200 meters along a straight circuit
- 5 minutes stretch
- * 1 x 200 meters along a straight track
- 5 minutes skips of several kinds
- * 2 sets of four triangles (6 sides of 8 meters each); recovery intervals: 20 seconds between two consecutive triangles and 4 minutes between the two sets
- hops (60 steps in total)
- * 2 sets of 5 50 meter running repetitions (recovery periods: 30 seconds between the repetitions and 2 minutes 30 seconds between the two sets)
- 1 short 'run there and back' (30 meters in total)
- * 2 sets of 150 meter 'sprint and release' exercise (alternate 15 m sprinting with 15 m running); 3 minutes interval between two consecutive 'sprint and release' activities
- hurdling: 4 sets of 6 high hurdles - standing jumps
- * 2 'run there and back' exercises (60 meters in total)

Example 4 It also includes hill running exercise; obviously, this is possible only if the hills are near the training field:
- * 1 set of 200 meter shuttle running exercise (50 meters long)
- 10 x half squat jumps
- 5 minutes walking (to reach the hills)
- * 4 60 meter hill running repetitions; 2 minutes 30 seconds recovery interval between two consecutive repetitions
- 5 minutes stretch
- * 2 sets of 3 70 meter 'sprint and release' running repetitions on hills (30 m sprinting + 10 m jogging + 30 m sprinting); recovery intervals: 2 minutes 30 seconds between two consecutive repetitions and 4 minutes between the two sets
- 5 minutes walking (to move to the training field)
- 5 minutes stretch
- * 1 200-meter 'sprint and release' exercise (alternate 12.5 sprinting with 12.5 m running)
- 5 minutes skips
- * 4 sets of (25 m + 35 m + 45 m) repetitions; during the recovery interval between two consecutive sprints, players jog so as to cover

the same distance of the sprint; players are divided into three groups: while one group are sprinting, the two others jog; therefore, there is one working period and two recovery intervals
- 5 minutes stretch
- * 2 'run there and back' exercises (72 meters in total); 60 seconds recovery interval between the two repetitions.

The Dietary Components of Endurance

There is no doubt that a proper diet can help to improve the athlete's performance in soccer. Having a suitable diet helps the player not only to prevent possible deficiencies and to maintain his ideal body weight (or better, not to exceed certain values of body fat concentration) but also to enhance his physical efficiency, especially in some particular situations and conditions. In particular, if we want to refer to the specific subject of this book, suitable dietary choices and combinations can improve soccer players' endurance during the course of a match.

In this chapter, I would like to specifically focus the attention on the following aspects:

- the possibility of feeding muscle glycogen stores by means of suitable dietary strategies; this is particularly important when two matches are played within a very short time;
- hydration immediately after the pre-match warm-up, during the recovery interval at half time and throughout the competition, if necessary; suitable hydration is fundamental especially if the levels of temperature, humidity and sun radiation in the air are particularly high;
- possible carbohydrate intake immediately before the match and at half time.

Feeding muscle glycogen stores

Research carried out by prof. Ekblom in 1986 proved that muscle glycogen concentration can directly influence the athlete's performance during a soccer match, especially in the second half. Glycogen is by far the most important source of energy for soccer players. It is a sort of starch, a polysaccharide consisting of a highly branched polymer of glucose (simple sugar). Glycogen stores are gradually broken down to glucose molecules which are used by muscle fibers to release energy. The higher the intensity at which muscles are working, the larger the amount of energy provided by glycogen stores. The lower the intensity of physical exercise, the more important the intervention of fatty acids, the other fuel that muscles generally use to release energy.

Soccer is a typical sports discipline where muscles mostly use glycogen as a source of energy, so it is important to remember that, due to significant depletion of muscle glycogen stores, the athlete's physical efficiency is seriously impaired: in particular, speed and endurance. This is why soccer players can considerably benefit if their muscle glycogen stores are full at the beginning of a competition, since the physical efficiency decreases significantly at the end of the first half if muscle glycogen concentration is rather low before the match.

There are some particular dietary strategies which allow the glycogen concentration to rise in muscles. In practice, players should eat foods high in carbohydrates - like bread, pasta, rice, bread sticks, fruit, vegetables (potatoes, in particular), desserts with no cream or custard, cookies and so forth - at the meals immediately preceding the match.

This does not mean that these meals should exclude foods rich in proteins and fats completely, only that these nutriments should be reduced to minimum quantities in favor of carbohydrates.

Since it takes at least 48 hours to replace muscle glycogen stores even when foods are properly chosen - if the diet is low in carbohydrates, it takes a much longer time - it is highly recommended that players follow some particular dietary suggestions during the couple of days preceding the competition, especially when the matches are very close to each other like in the case of midweek matches (when teams play on Tuesday and Thursday, for instance).

Breakfast: it can include citrus fruit juice, bread or toast with little marmalade or honey (no butter), wholemeal cereals, and tea or coffee (it is advisable to avoid white coffee, especially the day of the match since it takes hours to digest).

Lunch and dinner:

first courses: pasta, rice and vegetable soups are highly recommended; remember to reduce dressing to very minimum quantities, much less than in typical Italian cuisine; for instance, pasta and rice should be dressed with a spoonful of raw extra virgin olive oil and grated cheese.

main courses: they are typically rich in proteins and fats; therefore, too generous a portion should be avoided. The same is true for cheeses and cold cuts; meats should be cooked with no butter or oil (or with very minimum amounts) and fat should always be trimmed off; it is better to avoid eating the chicken skin, the white part of ham, fried foods and so forth.

vegetables: they are all recommended, both fresh and cooked, provided they are cooked with little fatty substance; it is advisable to avoid French fries, since it is much better to eat boiled potatoes flavored with a little oil and vinegar (or oil and lemon).

fruit: all fruits are highly recommended with the exception of oily dried fruits (like walnuts, hazel nuts, almonds, and peanuts). Remember that, as a rule, it is better to eat fruit far from the main meals (especially if one needs to digest more quickly).

dessert: sweets with cream or custard should be avoided completely; therefore, athletes should prefer fruits in syrup, fruit salad, pies and cakes low in fats, and sherbets.

bread: it is highly recommended as well as bread sticks, toast and crackers.

drinks: one glass of wine or beer is allowed at every meal; it is advisable to avoid drinking too many soft drinks high in sugar like colas, etc.; fruit shakes and juices are highly recommended.

In case two consecutive matches are play within less than 48 hours (which is likely to occur in some tournaments), it is even more important for players to quickly replace their muscle glycogen stores. Both sucrose - that is common table sugar - and glucose - a simple sugar which is also called dextrose - play a crucial role in feeding glycogen stores in muscles. In practice, I usually suggest that soccer players:

• drink orange juice immediately after the match; colas (which contain even higher sucrose concentrations) should be completely avoided since they usually contain a certain amount of caffeine, a substance which typically disturbs the synthesis of muscle glycogen;

• drink another can of juice 30 to 50 minutes later;

• eat a banana another 30 to 50 minutes later;

• eat foods high in carbohydrates (in particular at the meals between two consecutive matches), while always following the suggestions given above.

Hydration

When a player loses 2 to 3% of his total body weight in water while sweating, his physical efficiency is obviously impaired. This loss of water is especially large if the match is played in very sunny weather conditions characterized by high temperature and humidity. Remember that the percentage of water loss significantly affecting the athlete's physical efficiency is lower in non-trained or poorly trained individuals than in well-trained players who are accustomed to sweating profusely.

Sweating and gradual adaptation to sweating

Sweat is a weak solution of salts whose composition varies in relation to training and acclimation (see table 10.1). It is secreted by sweat glands in the skin and has a very similar ion concentration to blood plasma, which means it is an isotonic solution. However, while passing through glandular ducts, ion concentration and potassium concentration (even though to a smaller extent) considerably decrease due to gradual absorption of these substances. Therefore, the sweat poured out from the surface of the skin is hypotonic; sodium, chlorine, calcium and magnesium concentrations are even likely to be one third or one fourth that of plasma, while potassium concentration is very similar or just a little lower.

In the individual who practices for several days or a few weeks in weather conditions which make it very difficult for the body to remove heat (namely, high levels of temperature and/or humidity and/or sun radiation), there is a gradual process of adaptation to sweat production:

1 - ion concentration lowers (compare the values in the fourth and in the fifth column in table 10.1);
2 - sweat can reach a larger surface of the body skin;
3 - the amount of sweat secreted by the sweat glands per minute rises significantly.

If microclimatic conditions are equal, the first two factors help larger amounts of sweat secreted by the glands to evaporate from the skin. Since the sweat that cannot evaporate (for instance, the sweat which merely accumulates on the skin or soaks through the clothes when the surrounding air is saturated) is absolutely useless for thermo-regulation, these two factors are particularly beneficial since less sweat can be secreted, to take up the same amount of heat from the body. This consequently means a reduced loss of water and salts. The higher the relative humidity in the air, the smaller the amount of sweat which can evaporate through the skin. Obviously, the third factor also plays a very important role in regulating the body temperature.

Re-hydration

In very difficult weather conditions, well-trained and acclimatized individuals are very likely to lose similar amounts of sweat which directly impair their performances in a very short time (even several minutes, in some cases). This is why it would be necessary to promptly replace that loss of fluid, or, still better, to prevent such a loss from occurring. It is first of all important to remember that an individual can lose as much as 40 to 50 milliliters of water per minute of physical exercise through the skin and the respiratory apparatus, while his digestive system can provide the body with a smaller volume of fluid, that is 25 milliliters of water per minute at most.

Basically, re-hydration is limited by the time that fluids take to pass through the stomach and by the actual time that water takes to be completely absorbed by the intestine mucosa.

Very often, the first factor plays a crucial role in the process of re-hydration. It directly depends on the temperature of the fluid, on the total amount of fluid ingested at a time and on its carbohydrate and salt concentration. It is better to drink cold beverages: those whose temperature is below 15% can pass through the stomach much more easily; if their temperature is between 2.5% and 9%, the temperature of the stomach can drop considerably, thus enhancing gastric motility and taking up heat from the inner parts of the body. However, if the drink is too cold, cramp may occur. The ideal temperature of a drink is about 4 degrees centigrade.

As to the ideal amount of fluids players should ingest, in theory it should be about two thirds of a liter at a time, since this quantity is supposed to favor an increase in gastric pressure, thus helping part of the fluid to flow into the intestine. In this way, a larger volume of fluid would pass through the stomach. In practice, however, an excessive relaxation of the stomach brings about undesirable symptoms (like a sense of irritation). This is why it is advisable to drink only one glass at a time.

Pure water would be usually recommended, but some researchers believe that, for maximal absorption to be possible, it should contain minimum concentrations of sugar and salt (sodium, in particular), since both sugars and salts can 'drag' and therefore carry away

Salt Mineral	Extracellular Fluid	At rest	Non Athlete Acclimatized	Athlete Acclimatized
Sodium	3.25	1.85	1.38	0.92
Chlorine	3.70	3.10	1.50	1.00
Potassium	0.20	0.20	0.20	0.15
Calcium	0.10	0.04	0.04	0.03
Magnesium	0.04	0.01	0.01	0.01
TOTAL	7.29	5.20	3.13	2.11

Table 10.1
Mineral salts, in grams per liter, occurring in extracellular fluids, in the sweat of an individual at rest, in the sweat of a non-acclimatized athlete and, finally, in the sweat of a well-acclimatized athlete. Sodium and chlorine concentrations (as well as calcium and magnesium concentrations) in the sweat of a well acclimatized athlete are three to four times lower than extracellular fluids; on the contrary, potassium concentration is reduced only to a minimum extent.

water molecules when they are absorbed in the intestine mucosa.

In any case, sugar concentration should be very low: some scientists say that for water to flow through the stomach and be digested quickly it should not exceed 25 grams per liter of fluid. However, there are no particular problems up to 40 or 50 grams of sugar per liter of water.

Fructose is the best sugar for two reasons: first of all, a solution containing fructose passes through the stomach more quickly than a solution containing glucose (or dextrose) or sucrose (common table sugar); secondly, in order to penetrate the muscle fiber, fructose does not need insulin, whose concentration in the blood is always rather low when the athlete is performing physical activity at a high intensity.

A small amount of sugar dissolved in the drink may be useful since it helps to maintain glycemia at constant levels and also because it saves part of the glycogen stored in muscles. Nevertheless, only very minimum amounts of glycogen can be saved, since muscles can use up the quantity of sugar (25 to 50 grams) which was previously recommended per liter of fluid in a few minutes.

As for mineral salts, in the past athletes were usually advised to take special drinks consisting of common table salt dissolved in a little water during the competition. Fortunately, this habit has been completely abandoned today. Apart from causing serious heartburn in some individuals, it does not help to replace or prevent salt deficiency; on the contrary, it can even lay the basis for more serious disorders and greater imbalance, since sodium concentration in the sweat is much lower than in the blood. Therefore the body is deprived of larger quantities of water than of salts while sweating; consequently, if the athlete ingests much sodium and little water, he provides his body with a large amount of substance it has in excess and a minimum quantity of what it really lacks.

Obviously, when an athlete sweats profusely, his loss of salts may even account for a considerable percentage of the total amount of sodium occurring in his body. A small amount of sodium chloride can also be dissolved in the drinks that players usually take during the competition, but it should not exceed 2 grams per liter of beverage at most. Something similar could be said about the other electrolytes. In short, the athlete only needs to know that the drink for the match should contain a little salt and sugar. This is especially important when the main purpose is to replace the loss of water very quickly.

In short, the drinks especially prepared with salts are better than pure water during the course of the match, so the team should always take bottles to the playing field when weather conditions cause players to sweat profusely and they should also be readily available to the players during the pauses in the match. Those drinks especially designed for athletes should always be preferred. In the coldest periods of the year salt can be added to tea, even in larger amounts than in the hot season.

Pre-hydration

If players know or can anticipate that they are going to play in particular weather conditions causing profuse sweating (high temperature, humidity and sun radiation levels), they can seriously think of resorting to suitable pre-hydration, especially if they are not accustomed to these conditions.

In practice, pre-hydration consists in drinking two glasses (or even more, in some cases) of water or saline solutions during the 10 to 15 minutes immediately preceding the match. In this way, the body cannot lose that amount of fluid in urine, since there is not enough time. When there is an excess of water in the body because the individual has drunk too much or has eaten foods rich in water, the hypophysis promptly reduces the release of the antidiuretic hormone into the blood. Since high levels of antidiuretic hormone mean that little urine is passed from the body, low antidiuretic hormone concentrations obviously mean that a lot of urine is passed. This is why - in standard conditions - the body typically produces large volumes of urine when much fluid is ingested. Don't forget that:

- it takes several minutes for this particular mechanism of the antidiuretic hormone to be effectively activated;
- when the individual is performing physical exercise, his body stops (or considerably reduces) the production of urine in order to save water, which it will obviously need to form sweat;
- if the body is supplied with suitable amounts of water less than 10 to 15 minutes before the match or after the warm-up period (pre-hydration), there is not enough time for the antidiuretic hormone mechanism to be activated before kick-off, so the player can start playing the match with an extra supply of water in his body.

However, it is better for athletes to experience pre-hydration in training sessions before adopting it in official competitions.

Alcohol and thermal balance

If players can anticipate that they are going to sweat profusely during the match, they had better avoid drinking alcohol the night before. Alcohol directly upsets the body's thermal balance. The negative effects are particularly felt at two different levels: on one side, this substance causes the hypophysis to release the antidiuretic hormone in lower concentrations and therefore stimulate urine production, thus depriving the body of a certain volume of water which it would especially need to produce considerable amounts of sweat. On the other hand, alcohol directly affects the mechanisms responsible for regulating the body temperature and therefore impairs their efficiency, thus making it much more difficult for the body to remove excess heat.

10.3 Is carbohydrate intake immediately before the match and at half time really helpful?

According to Sassi and Somenzini (1992), there are valid reasons to believe that soccer players can really benefit from suitable carbohydrate intake before a match. Research carried out by prof. Mukle proved that the performances of the analyzed team were much better - especially in the second half of the matches - in the 10 matches when players were previously administered carbohydrates than in the 10 matches when they were not. Soccer players benefit from ingesting suitable mixtures of fructose and maltodextrins - one gram per every kilogram of the athlete's body weight. Maldodextrin intake both before and during the match helps to save muscle glycogen stores on one side, while also enhancing the athlete's performance. On the other hand, fructose (the amount should never exceed 40 to 50 grams) could be considered as the best source of energy and is highly recommended immediately before the match, since it has no negative effects on glycemia due to minor stimulation of insulin.

11

The Psychological Components of Endurance

In this short chapter, I would like to especially focus the attention on the relations existing between the human psyche and physical endurance. The willingness and the capability to carry out any kind of physical activity are certainly influenced by several psychological factors. Endurance performances are particularly affected compared to other activities, because they typically imply higher levels of fatigue.

When the player is reluctant to endurance training

The first subject that I would like to deal with is the players' willingness to face endurance training. It is true that that some players consider this kind of work as something punitive. But I think this is also due to the fact that, in most youth teams, coaches usually punish their young players by making them run around the playing field or run 250 meter repetitions when they behave badly. This is a counterproductive habit, since it encourages young players to identify punishment with endurance training. Furthermore, it is also proven that those who have decided to practice an individual endurance sport (like middle distance running and all the competitions beyond 200 meters in swimming, for instance; not to mention marathon, cross-country skiing or triathlon) are much more distinctly accustomed to accepting the fatigue of training than their fellow athletes playing team sports, where endurance is just one of the several qualities they need to enhance.

Obviously, the coach plays a crucial role in this situation, since his constant intervention, his coaching methods and his approach to his players can directly influence his athletes' approach to training and also help them to understand how important it is to work in the best way possible. If the coach is the first person who believes that endurance exercise is not really beneficial, he will unconsciously convey his firm belief in the uselessness of that work to his players, even through non-verbal communication, producing a reaction of rejection to endurance training by his players.

When one team can endure the competition more than the opposition

The importance of the final score can significantly enhance players' strengths and endurance capacities during the match. If players do not feel the need to struggle either for winning the league or to avoid being bottom or to achieve other important goals, as it typically happens in some matches at the end of the league, they tend to lower the intensity of their physical efforts as soon as they feel the first symptoms of fatigue (even the weakest ones). Consequently, they sprint less, do not fight to intercept passes or to win possession of the ball when it is between them and their opponents, do not sprint to support their teammates in possession of the ball and so forth. In practice, 'they do not play without the ball'. In short, they appear as if they lack endurance.

However, the opposite is not always true. If one team has valid reasons to fight and is therefore highly motivated, while the opposition has no motivation at all, the general impression is that the players on the former team are better trained and can endure physical activity more than their opponents. On the other hand, if they play against another highly-motivated side - and fortunately, this happens quite often, otherwise the spectacular nature of soccer would be shot down completely - all those basic biological factors (resulting either from nature directly, or from carrying out special training) which allow players to play the whole match at high intensity are of critical importance.

A player once told me he failed to maintain the rhythm and pace of his opponents when playing off for promotion; and he also told me what happened at a certain moment during the match: "It was evident that our opponents were better trained than us from the point of view of physical endurance; what I personally thought at a certain moment during the match - and what my teammates also thought, of course - was: 'If you really want to win, then win!'. We won that match and were finally promoted to a higher division".

In other words, I would say that both the psychological disposition and the physical willingness to run and work hard are vital characteristics of an athlete.

11.3 When players reduce the intensity of physical exercise at the very first symptoms of fatigue

Inborn skills - that is all those abilities inherited from birth - are particularly important not only because they allow some individuals to be naturally superior to others, but also because - assuming training is equal - naturally skillful players can improve in a much more evident way than their fellow athletes. Apart from this important aspect, I would also like to point out that those who usually engage more seriously and work hard in training sessions and matches, generally tend to improve more than those who apply themselves and work little (as the experience on the playing field clearly teaches us). Americans are used to saying: 'No pain, no gain', which means that no real improvement is possible without fatigue. Those who typically reduce the intensity of physical exercise when the first symptoms of fatigue appear while undertaking endurance training generally improve very little or do not enhance their endurance capabilities at all. For 1,000 or 800 meter aerobic running repetitions to be highly effective, for instance, athletes should run at a speed beyond their anaerobic threshold velocity (3 to 5% faster is optimal). However, if they ran at a sensibly lower speed, they would suffer less from fatigue, but the positive effects of endurance training would be considerably poorer. The same is also true for lactic acid training: if the intensity of physical exercise is reduced so that very little lactate or no lactate at all is produced in muscles, players would not really benefit from this kind of work and this would obviously bring about little improvement. Similar things can also be said for special high-intensity training situations with the ball, like 1 v 1, 2 v 2, and so forth.

However, once again I would like to underline that the symptoms of fatigue do not necessarily mean real improvement if the physical input is not good from the qualitative point of view and insufficient at a quantitative level. In short, walking for two or three hours considerably stimulates fatigue, but does not bring about any adaptation or improvement in the body which can positively affect the players' performance in the match. Remember that if the athlete does not get tired and does not feel the symptoms of fatigue when athletic exercise is properly carried out, the saying 'No pain (= no fatigue), no gain (= no improvement)' is absolutely true.

12

The Effects of Endurance Training on Sprinting

Many people still believe that it is useless - or even complete-ly wrong - to encourage soccer players to enhance their aerobic capacities by means of special endurance training, but I believe that most of them think like that because they do not really know that kind of work. I have noted that most of them have never had any experience as a coach in those sports where the aer-obic components of endurance are fundamental; but, above all, I have specifically noticed that whenever they discuss this important subject, they always make wrong references. One of the main argu-ments which they typically insist on to defend their ideas is that aer-obic conditioning negatively affects some special qualities which are of critical importance in soccer, like sprint and muscular explosive power. On the other hand, when they are asked to describe which kind of exercise really brings about such deterioration, they invari-ably refer to jogging, a conditioning activity which is no longer used to improve the aerobic components of endurance in modern soccer.

In reality, I think that workouts especially designed to enhance aerobic capacities, as discussed in chapters five, six and seven, may impair some other physical qualities, but this risk is minimal when the athlete trains properly.

Sprint and endurance: mutual conflict?

Ruben Dario Oliva used to say that there are such unlucky dogs that they have both fleas and lice. But there are also such lucky athletes whose both sprinting skills and endurance capacitates are far above the average and who can further enhance their sprint and endurance by means of special training.

In junior or senior high school, as well as in many soccer teams there are players who can outrun nearly all their friends both over a very short distance such as 20 or 30 meters, and over longer distances, such as 3,000 meters. Those players usually have a very harmonious locomotor apparatus and no fat in excess. In general, their muscles are not particularly developed and have neither stocky figures (as is usually the case in quick persons who are not capable of endurance as is typical), nor thin physiques and poor muscle mass (as is typical in those who are capable of endurance, but are not very quick). Roberto Sassi once told me that when he subjected Torino's Gian Luigi Lentini to a series of special tests some years ago, he found that the player - who was very young at that time - was excellent from the point of view of strength, quickness and endurance.

By contrast, it is absolutely wrong to believe that every individual can be either quick or capable of physical endurance in relation to the features prevailing in his muscle fibers. Pale muscle fibers are supposed to enhance quickness, while red muscle fibers would favor endurance. There has always been great confusion about this. It is proven that pale fibers account for more than 50% of the total muscle fibers in sprinters of worldwide renown, while red fibers usually account for about two thirds of the muscle fibers in top-class long-distance runners. On the other hand it is excessively superficial to believe that the athletic features of an individual directly result from one single factor: the percentage of his muscle fibers. Obviously, several important components are involved, starting from biological, technical, psychological aspects and so forth...

But there is something more: not only are there individuals who are much quicker and capable of endurance than others, but it is also possible to enhance both sprinting and endurance at the same time. When I was working as fitness coach at Varese soccer club and subjected the most promising young players to special post-season training for a few weeks, I realized that most players significantly improved their performances in 50 and 300 meter repetitions in the Abalakov Test and in long distance running at the end of that extra conditioning period compared to the results recorded at the beginning of the season. Many fitness coaches, especially those who work with youth teams, know that their players can generally improve their performances both in endurance and strength tests during the course of the pre-season conditioning period and that these improvements are definitely more significant than those resulting from physical development.

By means of special training it is possible to work on muscle fibers' metabolic and mechanical features and on several structures and functions of the whole body as well. The several kinds of adjustments occurring in the body as a consequence of athletic conditioning are biologically based - in most cases, at least - on the synthesis of new structures, like myofibrils, mitochondria and so on. This means that the synthesis of highly-specific molecules is the consequence of a particular training input. Sometimes, the same change occurring in the body can have both positive and negative effects. For instance, training can make a fiber much stronger and therefore increase its volume. In this case, it takes a much longer time for oxygen to flow from the capillary to the mitochondrion. However, if conditioning methods and activities are properly combined (though I have to admit this is rather difficult), it is possible for the athlete to experience those physical adjustments which can enhance two different qualities at the same time, like strength and endurance. In short, these two important capacities are not in such a deep contrast with each other, as we have often read.

When one particular physical capacity is impaired

When a certain physical activity is lacking, any organ or tissue obviously loses most of the features it had previously acquired by carrying out that particular exercise, which means that physical adaptation gradually disappears. In short, lack of special training - or the sensible decrease in physical exercise from the quantitative point of view - is the main reason why one particular capacity is gradually impaired and the performance is consequently affected. For instance, if the training specifically focuses on strength workouts and completely neglects endurance, this inevitably results in a gradual deterioration of endurance capacities; viceversa, it is obvious that strength decreases if the conditioning method only concentrates on endurance training.

But there is something more. It may happen that, in the same team, strength levels decrease less in a group of players who have been completely at rest (while on vacation, for instance) than in another group of players who have done light running exclusively over the same period of time. This especially happens when physical exercise is protracted for extended periods of time and in case of frequent conditioning sessions.

On the other hand, it is proven that strength can be considerably enhanced in a group of players who only carry out special strength exercise than in another group of athletes who combine the same strength training with several light running sessions throughout the week. Similar situations - maybe with less evident differences - may also occur when the target capacity which should be finally measured is endurance, while strength exercise is only carried out by one of the two groups.

I believe that there is a clear explanation to all of this; I also think this explanation should be understood by all those who are somehow involved in soccer where several physical attributes all play an important role and should therefore be properly trained at the same time. I would portray the situation by trying to condense such important and complex subjects into a few lines, as follows:

- particular changes occur in the fibers of working muscles which promptly activate testosterone and all the other hormones having 'anabolic' effects, that is the hormones which help the synthesis of new proteins (contractile proteins in the specific case of strength) from molecules or simple precursors in the fiber itself. In other words, the anabolic hormones (those produced by the body) occurring in working muscle fibers activate the process by which the fibers themselves increase in volume: in particular, the content of myofibrils (the structures responsible for muscle contraction) increases significantly and directly causes muscle fibers to become stronger;

- by contrast, 'catabolic' hormones act on all the several muscles in the body, that is both on working muscles and on those which are not involved in physical exercise and are therefore at rest. Catabolic hormones favor a process opposite to that of the anabolic hormone mechanism. They are responsible for the metabolic breakdown of large molecules to smaller ones, thus bringing about a decrease in the volume of muscle fibers and, consequently, in strength.

A considerable increase in catabolic hormone concentration is very likely to occur in athletes who usually go running for extended periods of time several times a week. Such hormones directly act on all muscle fibers, thus impairing their strength. If the athlete wants to prevent such a deterioration, not only does he need to stimulate that physical attribute by carrying out the same amount of work which would have been able to maintain his strength at constant levels if he had not been running, but he also needs to increase physical exercise: only in this way can 'anabolic' effects (the synthesizing of new molecules) counterbalance the 'catabolic' ones (the breakdown of large molecules).

It is absolutely absurd to state that specific training, which can significantly enhance a physical capacity that is prerequisite in soccer, should be avoided only because it is supposed to have negative effects on other abilities. In my opinion, it is much more reasonable to find the best method to suitably 'measure out' that kind of work and help to counterbalance positive and negative effects, so that the benefits can prevail over drawbacks. In the case of special exercise for the several components of endurance, and for peripheral aerobic components, in particular (see chapter 6) I think it is enough to also include quickness, agility and strength activities in the same training session, or in the same week conditioning plan.

13

Endurance Training
All Year Round

S occer players should train endurance not only during the pre-season conditioning period, but all year round. Obviously, endurance training during the season will be different from the conditioning methods specifically used in the pre-season. Both the quality and the quantity will also vary from one training session to another more than in the pre-season. It is extremely important for players to practice endurance all year round, which means also while on vacation - even though to a smaller extent.

The importance of practicing endurance all year round

Most coaches in Italian soccer understand the real importance of endurance training in the pre-season. However, there are still many coaches who do not realize how important it is to practice endurance during the course of the soccer season as well, or simply believe that it is sufficient to plan 'booster workouts' during the season breaks. I would like to underline that 'booster workouts' are certainly of critical importance since they are not going to play the following week-end.

Nevertheless, 'booster workouts' are not enough: in short, specific endurance training should be protracted throughout the soccer season. When some particular capacities (including endurance components) are not thoroughly trained for a few weeks, they inevitably tend to deteriorate. If the athlete resorts to heavy specific workloads to enhance his endurance levels, he needs to work still harder in order to maintain the level he has gradually reached than he would need if he had practiced little and poorly previously, with poor improvement of his endurance components. Those who were used to considering the match as the only way to gradually improve their endurance capacities from the very beginning of the pre-season training period on, only needed to play once a week to maintain those low endurance levels which they had reached. By contrast, those who progressively enhance the aerobic and lactic acid components of endurance up to high levels by means of specific athletic conditioning, run the risk of having those components rapidly deteriorate if they do not continue to train with adequate workloads.

Why are in-season athletic conditioning methods different from pre-season training?

In modern soccer, endurance is not usually trained during the course of the season in the same way it is practiced in the pre-season training period, since there are several differences both from the quantitative and the qualitative point of view. Maybe, those differences will be less marked in the future; both conditioning methods and athletes' disposition (physical and psychological) to receive them have undergone considerable changes in the last few years.

However, there are still significant differences today and there are also several reasons which can justify them.

First of all, it is important to remember that, during the pre-season training period, players are generally more inclined to work harder than throughout the season. Furthermore, the pre-season is undoubtedly very short if it is compared to the time players really need to develop the most important athletic capacities, to optimum levels following reasonable gradual training methods. This is why massive workloads are used in this conditioning period and, very often, they are even higher than those which should be applied when the reference is made to the players' poor efficiency at the very beginning of the season. Consequently, the symptoms of fatigue easily appear, which require long recovery intervals and tend to impair players' performances. Lackluster performances and loss of physical efficiency resulting from hard work are usually accepted in soccer only in this particular period.

During the season, by contrast, certain training methods and workloads should be completely avoided when matches are scheduled: the player's performance would be seriously impaired if he cannot perfectly recover from fatigue which is the consequence of strenuous exercise during the course of the week. On the other hand, it is also advisable to vary the conditioning activities to avoid the negative effects which may result from monotonous exercise throughout the season.

Considering all these important factors, one could think that the main goal of training of endurance components during the season is to maintain the levels players have gradually reached in the pre-season conditioning period. As far as the aerobic components of endurance are concerned, statistical information resulting from the times recorded in running repetitions (over a distance of 1,000 meters, for example) or from the results of the Conconi and Sassi Test and the Cooper Test, shows that some players - the youngest, in particular - can still improve if they practice thoroughly. As to the lactic acid components of endurance (which are peculiar to soccer players), I feel players can constantly enhance them during the first months of the season, provided that they practice regularly. Even though I have no data and figures which can prove such an improvement, I firmly believe that players' recovery capacities between two consecutive lactic acid activities tend to become increasingly shorter. The fact that losses of speed in the Capanna and Sassi shuttle run tests are more frequent in the first trials than in the last ones, could indicate (even if indirectly) that the lactic acid mechanism is much more efficient.

The week microcycle in soccer training

Eugenio Fascetti suggests diversifying training methods and personalizing conditioning workouts in the training sessions immediately following the match. He suggests that those who play the whole match on Sundays should practice differently during the week from those who do not play at all (or only play for a very short time). In particular, the Tuscan coach suggests:

- aerobic repetitions on Mondays (the first sessions in the week) and technical and tactical exercise on Tuesdays (the second session) for the athletes who did not play the Sunday match or only played a few minutes;
- a warm down session on Mondays, (since this should be their day off, every player should practice by himself), and aerobic repetitions on Tuesdays for those who played the whole Sunday match;
- lactic acid exercise on Wednesday mornings for both groups.

Those who played 90 minutes on Sunday generally find it very difficult to work hard on Monday, since their muscles are still very heavy and their physical efficiency has not recovered completely. On Tuesday, they can begin to handle strenuous and rather demanding exercise and most of them can perform aerobic repetitions or similar workouts. The Wednesday training session is the ideal period for lactic acid activities and I have also realized that players can endure lactic acid exercise both in the morning and in the afternoon, provided that athletic conditioning alternates with specific technical and tactical practice aimed at clear goals.

If this can be considered the basic training master plan for the week microcycle during the season, I believe that it is sometimes extremely helpful - from the psychological point of view, at least - to include some variations.

As to amateur players who usually practice only twice a week and need to carry out specific endurance training in both sessions, the conditioning microcycle could develop as follows:

- aerobic exercise in the first session and lactic acid workouts in the second one if the two training sessions are held on Tuesdays and Thursdays;
- lactic acid exercise in the first session and aerobic activities in the second if players practice on Wednesdays and Fridays; by Wednesday the body has already recovered from the fatigue resulting from the Sunday match and is able to work at high intensity, while aerobic exercise - which requires shorter recovery intervals than lactic acid exercise - can also be included in the Friday session.

For those training less frequently, aerobic exercise can be planned both at the beginning and at the end of the session, while lactic acid workouts should be suggested in the last part of the session, preferably after technical practice.

Diversifying endurance training throughout the season

The conditioning master plans of some particular sports include two or three microcycles of intense exercise ('heavy workload') and one microcycle characterized by light exercise (a sort of 'warm down' practice). In soccer, some coaches also adopt these 'three + one' (three weeks of hard work and one of light exercise) or 'two + one' (two weeks of heavy workloads and one of warm down) conditioning methods.

The warm down microcycle is undoubtedly beneficial in some situations, but it can be highly harmful in some other cases. In general, I would say that the warm down microcycle can be helpful:

For psychological reasons: if players are heavily involved in strenuous exercise for a few days or weeks and such hard work heavily affects their bodies and their minds (also because it sometimes forces them to give up most of their leisure activities), they can usually accept making sacrifices and working hard for another few days provided a real recovery period will soon follow;

For physical reasons: in some situations, it is fundamental to reduce workloads for a few days due to purely physical reasons; for instance, in order to help muscles restore their full efficiency and freshness, to allow endocrine glands to recover completely, to allow for the reduction of inflammation in tendons or ligaments and so forth.

Sometimes, the positive effects of a warm down week combine together. Imagine an amateur player who - in order to practice thoroughly - cannot go to bed early, or can never go to the disco or to the cinema; or suffers from acute knee pain. This player needs to recover from fatigue due to the intense rhythms of his life (also resulting from his work and daily activities, above all) and will undoubtedly benefit from sleeping more or going out and enjoying himself.

On the other hand, it is obvious that those who are not heavily committed in any activity (neither at a physical nor a psychological level) and maybe consider the training session as a really enjoyable moment in the day, do not need any warm down microcycle. It would be senseless to ask them to reduce their workloads during the training session, since they could even consider such a reduction more or less as a sort of punishment.

The warm down week also has its drawbacks:

- first of all, it inevitably brings about a reduction (qualitative and/or quantitative) in training; I would say that - in light of the overall effects on the athlete's body - all the other conditions being equal, such a reduction can be considered positively only if it helps to improve the athlete's performance and conditioning from the qualitative and/or quantitative point of view in the weeks immediately preceding or following the warm down period;
- practical experience proves that, when players go through a week of light exercise (specifically if workloads are reduced by more than 35 to 40%), their performances in the Sunday match are usually lackluster and poor from the physical point of view.

For all these reasons, it is advisable neither to plan 'three + one' or

'two + one' conditioning macrocycles or those involving considerable warm down exercise in the last week before the beginning of
the season, nor to suggest those training methods exclusively to the
teams who usually practice hard. Furthermore, I personally believe
that, from the purely physical point of view, even athletic conditioning of most professional soccer teams is never so demanding as
to make warm down sessions absolutely necessary. Most problems
develop at the psychological level. Therefore, the coach is responsible for constantly monitoring the situation - specifically focusing his
attention on his players' psychological involvement - and deciding
whether to reduce workloads for the whole group or for single players for a particular week. This does not mean that the coach should
not always diversify specific conditioning workouts for the various
components of endurance from one week to another to avoid the
risk of monotonous practice - as was pointed out earlier.

Is it really advisable to reduce workloads in the spring?

One basic rule which most soccer coaches comply with is to drasti-
cally reduce workloads in soccer players' athletic conditioning when
spring starts. The quality of training also varies, in the sense that
sprints and rapidity exercise are usually preferred to prolonged aerobic exercise.

In my opinion, this training method is absolutely wrong, specifically because it does not take into proper account the problem of
thermal balance in the human body and the way in which the body
adapts to particular environmental conditions.

It is in spring that soccer players generally find it more difficult to
remove heat from their bodies because they are playing in weather
conditions that are very different from those which they had been
used to until just a few days before (increased air temperature and
sun radiation in particular). In such weather conditions, apart from
eliminating the few or several thousands of kilocalories produced in
his muscles ('metabolic heat'), the athlete shall also remove from his
body the calories corresponding to the heat provided by sun radiation ('heat of radiation'). Otherwise, if the body cannot remove such
heat, the inner body temperature may rise above the basal level (37
degrees centigrade) and gradually impair any physical performance.
In practice, the athlete is forced to reduce his movements significantly.

By following the standard criteria of athletic conditioning or by reducing training workloads - according to the common rule which many coaches still comply with, as was pointed out earlier - for a few weeks players inevitably have serious difficulties during the course of the match, since their bodies are accustomed to working in low temperature and low radiation weather conditions, which are typical of the winter season.

By contrast, if they practice in hot weather conditions, they can acclimate more easily and therefore adapt quite rapidly to working in particular situations where their bodies need to remove much heat. Remember that this important adaptation is mainly connected to those factors which were previously discussed in chapter ten (paragraph 10.2.1, in particular), that is the capacity of the body to produce more sweat which can finally evaporate from the skin and take up more heat through the convection mechanism.

According to Astrand and Rohdal (1970) '.... most adaptations occur within 4 to 7 days from the first exposure of the body to hot weather conditions, while the body is completely acclimated within 12 to 14 days; even everyday exposure to hot weather for relatively short periods of time will be somehow beneficial....'. According to those authors, 50 minutes' exercise every day with no pauses at all is sufficient to bring about such adaptations in the body. Well-trained individuals can better acclimate to hot weather, but training which involves little production of sweat is not enough to favor those important physical adjustments which are necessary to remove from the body increasingly large amounts of sweat per minute.

Running is a very useful conditioning method for soccer players to stimulate their muscles to produce metabolic heat (both in the unit of time and as an absolute value), provided they run for a few kilometers at a sufficiently fast speed. If they run at too slow a pace (less than 10 km/h, for example) and there is no sun radiation at all, the amount of heat to remove from the body is definitely insufficient for real important adaptations to occur.

For suitable acclimation to be possible, training should include 15-20 minutes' (in the first session) to 30 35 minutes' (after a few sessions) running involving 40 60 second sprints every 3 to 6 minutes. Then, it can include either athletic conditioning or technical and tactical exercise (always causing players to sweat profusely), in relation to the main goals the coach wants to achieve in that particular training session. On the basis of what we have already underlined before, total exercise carried out with no pauses in-between (or with very short recovery intervals) and at a good intensity should last more than 50 minutes.

However, it is fundamental to remember that, in order to avoid harmful water and salt deficiencies before the match, players should ingest suitable fluid supplements after the above-mentioned training sessions and also avoid exposure to excess heat on the two or three days immediately preceding the match. This obviously means that training sessions should be rather short and/or not excessively demanding from the physical point of view in case of high temperature and sun radiation levels, in particular.

In conclusion, is it absolutely wrong to reduce the duration of conditioning sessions as spring is gradually approaching. On the contrary, until matches follow one another at standard intervals (that is every Sunday, for instance), players can endure long training sessions in the first part of the week (that is until Wednesday or Thursday), which also cause them to sweat profusely. Only in the second part of the week, by contrast, should the duration of conditioning sessions be reduced. This is the best way for a soccer player to gradually acclimate according to the basic principles of physiology.

13.6 Is it really helpful to introduce extra aerobic exercise every week throughout the season?

For those teams which usually take three training sessions a week at least, in my opinion it would be really helpful to introduce another aerobic exercise during the course of the week. In the case of professional teams, the Thursday session (or the Friday session, as prof. Gigi Asnaghi generally proposes) would be ideal to suggest extra aerobic workouts. This kind of exercise could also be planned at the end of a session focused on soccer technique and tactics or in the middle of it. I am now going to suggest some basic examples of aerobic exercise (other workouts can be planned according to the fitness coach's personal creativeness). The following suggestions share various great advantages: the activities can be practiced in a very short time (less than a quarter of an hour, in general), do not require considerable physical and psychological effort (unlike the workouts suggested on Tuesday) and, consequently, can be 'absorbed' quite rapidly (see table 13.1, which also shows the best way to combine these activities with those in the first aerobic session):

A - 2 to 3 minutes aerobic shuttle running; the players line up along one goal line, run about 100 meters up to the opposite goal line, run back and restart again for 2 to 3 minutes; every player should run at a speed slightly above his own anaerobic threshold pace (even though the performance is not timed, every player should be able to concentrate on his speed and thoroughly assess the rhythm). This means that the athletes who can run faster in aerobic repetitions can gradually outdistance the others, or those who can run slower are very likely not to run along the whole length of the field, but turn around a few (or several) meters before the goal line (this happens quite often). This exercise should be carried out once or twice.

B - 5 minutes circuit training; the players run around the playing field, standing a few meters apart; when they arrive behind each one of the two goals (or in any other position of the field), they are asked to perform some specific tasks, which vary from one lap to another. These specific activities should always be performed at such an intensity which brings about an increase in heart rate: for instance, they may be asked to jump over low hurdles, make a slalom through the cones, run backward, run sideways, skip, promptly turn around and so forth; this circuit training should be repeated twice, at least.

C - 4 to 6 minutes running from one post to another; the players run all together within the playing field; 12 to 16 posts of two different colors (white and red, for example) are positioned along the side lines, the goal lines and randomly on the field. Every player moves to touch one white and one red post alternately and can run back to the first one only after touching all the posts; the exercise is protracted for about 4 to 6 minutes, once or twice;

D - 10 minutes free running ('short and fast' in soccer); all the players run freely for about 10 minutes all over the field, ignoring each other; they move simultaneously in any part of the field (or even in a much larger area) and pay particular attention - as Umberto Borino says - to the symptoms of fatigue their bodies promptly communicate (breathing rate and depth, heavy muscles, general feeling of difficulty and so forth). One possible variation suggested by Borino: players are asked to reproduce the same movements they would make in a match at a steadily intense rhythm, in their usual positions or in other roles; one single repetition per training session is usually enough.

E - speed variations to promptly occupy free spaces; the players run freely all over the field at a speed similar to the basic speed of a

	first aerobic session (on Tuesday, in general)	second aerobic session (on Thursday or Friday, in general)
Week A	timed running repetitions over 1,000 meters	3 to 5 minutes aerobic circuit training including various activities
Week B	To 300 meter running repetitions with recovery intervals of about 20 to 40 seconds	10 minutes 'sort and fast' running
Week C	Running repetitions over distances; Of about 400 and 900 meters, or run tests for set times (12 min)	distances (3,000 meters) aerobic running slalom through the posts
Week D	2 to 30 minutes fartlek with different inputs of about 40 secs.	2 to 3 minutes aerobic shuttle running

Table 13.1
Some examples of double aerobic exercise in the same week; one of the two sessions (the first one, in general) involves heavier workloads, while the other (on Thursday or Friday, in general) includes lighter exercise.

fartlek exercise of the same duration; when the coach gives the signal, they sprint for about 30 seconds at a speed slightly above their personal threshold velocity, while also trying to occupy free spaces in a very reasonable manner; 2 minutes' recovery intervals at a slower pace; the overall duration is about 12 minutes.

F - speed variations with prompt chase; the players run in pairs around the perimeter of the playing field; the pairs stand 5 to 10 meters apart; at regular intervals - 5 to 8 seconds, for example - the two players heading the line gradually increase their speed, sprint to chase after their teammates and bring up the rear of the line; this exercise should last about 10 minutes.

G - speed variations and turns (this exercise is suggested by Umberto Borino); these players start like in the previous exercise, but in this situation, when the coach gives the signal, the two players heading the line promptly turn around and change their pace; they bring up the rear of the line when they cross their teammates; the exercise lasts about 10 minutes.

Endurance training in summer

Up to 20 years ago, soccer players were not accustomed to

practicing in the off season. In some cases they were even dissuaded from playing tennis or swimming. What's more, they did not carry out any physical activity at all. Consequently, some of them had a few kilograms of fat in excess (even more than ten, in some cases) and their bodies were completely rusty when the pre-season training period began. Their total inactivity was very often encouraged by the ideas of their soccer coaches, who firmly believed that the season had already 'worn out' their bodies. Many coaches were convinced that physical exercise inevitably brought about an impairment of physical efficiency and, in order to support their theory, they usually made a comparison to racing cars, which need to be completely re-built after a 'Grand Prix'.

As years went by, things began to change gradually and today most players (probably all, or nearly all the professional athletes playing the highest divisions - in the Italian Serie A and B, for instance) are always very active while on vacation. Not only do they play tennis and swim, but also row, go running, cycle, play volleyball, five-a-side soccer and so forth. In practice, they try to do everything possible to be in constant motion. Furthermore, during the 10 to 15 days immediately preceding the pre-season training camp, many players are still preparing for pre-season training, following specific tables and conditioning plans their coaches give them before leaving on vacation.

Specific athletic conditioning carried out during the summer period should be aimed at:
- helping the athlete to maintain his overall physical efficiency;
- helping the player to keep his body weight constant;
- preparing the body for pre-season training.

In my opinion, the last goal is of critical importance. As was pointed out in paragraph 13.2, training workloads are heavy during the course of the pre-season. If the body efficiency is very poor in that period - in particular, if the athlete is not thoroughly accustomed to enduring fatigue - it will take a few or even several weeks for the player to 'digest' those workloads and completely recover from fatigue.

As to the various components of endurance, I firmly believe that soccer players would considerably benefit if they understood how helpful it is for them to maintain their physical efficiency at constant levels while on vacation. This is why I usually suggest that soccer players combine standard athletic conditioning for the summer period (which is based on stretching and running and sometimes includes hops and sprints) with:

- aerobic running repetitions once a week; for instance, 3 x 500 or 600 meter repetitions (obviously, it is not necessary to measure the distance very accurately; what is really important is to run at a speed which is very close or even slightly above one's personal anaerobic threshold pace, so that the body gradually gets accustomed to enduring fatigue), in the woods or on the beach, if possible (remember that it is always fundamental to wear the right shoes!);
- lactic acid exercise once a week; for instance, players can perform 3 or 4 running repetitions over distances of about 200 meters, at a speed which directly brings about a sense of fatigue typical of the situations when a certain amount of lactic acid is produced in muscles.

If soccer players can take four conditioning sessions of the first kind and four of the second type during their one month's holiday, their endurance mechanisms will be undoubtedly highly efficient at the beginning of the pre-season training period.

14

Prolonged Running

When soccer players were not used to running

When I began to work as a soccer fitness coach in the early 70s, the expression 'athletic conditioning' (in reality, the right definition was 'gymnastic-athletic conditioning' at that time) referred to specific pre-season training which mainly consisted of two elements: long walking in the woods and gymnastics. When the season started, walking was excluded from the conditioning plan, while gymnastics remained. I clearly remember that I had the greatest difficulties in suggesting different running styles. In order to gradually 'train' soccer players to running and therefore prepare them for actual soccer performances (that is the most intense and suitable workouts to bring about those physical adaptations which help to be highly efficient during the course of the match), I used the training method which I still consider as the most effective in achieving this important goal: running. It is fundamental to underline that running has become a very popular activity which is performed by individuals of all age groups in the last few years. At that time, on the contrary, nobody was running, with the exception of track and field athletes (who were generally youths, since 'master/senior athletes' did not exist like today).

I remember that at the very beginning of my career as fitness coach in Varese Calcio in 1972, many players - most of whom were about 19 to 20 year olds - had great difficulties in running for even a very few kilometers with no pauses during the pre-season training period, since they had never run any substantial distance before. In particular, in the second or third session, one of them (who then became a top-class player in the Italian Serie A) suddenly burst into tears because he was completely tired out 10 or 12 minutes later! And they were certainly running at a slower speed than 5 minutes per kilometer.... He clearly told me he was sure he could not endure the 20 minutes' running that my training plan included for the following session. In reality, within a few days, he gradually got accustomed to running and other running styles as well. Furthermore, he practiced so thoroughly in that period that he even changed his playing features completely: from a nearly motionless attacking player he gradually turned to be a real linkman who ran upward and backward on the flank of the field over and over again during the course of the match.

I also remember that a new 20 year old player arrived at Varese Calcio two or three years later. He had grown in the most prestigious Italian youth teams, always fighting to be one of the top players in the Italian Under 16 and Under 18 leagues, and had also a few Champions' League appearances. Nevertheless, he was also infamous for his lack of physical endurance. When I first asked him what kind of exercise he was used to taking to remedy his personal deficiency, I immediately found out that he had never run for more than 400 meters on end in his life!

What soccer players generally do by themselves while on vacation today, and what thousands of people are used to doing (without feeling neither heroes nor real athletes) - that is running for a few kilometers - was absolutely unusual at that time, so exceptional that the subject had to be discussed with a certain emphasis.

Up to twenty years ago, this conditioning method was unknown and great emphasis had to be laid on it. Then, people began to overuse or use running in the wrong way, since they believed it could improve all the possible components of endurance and, consequently, running was gradually seen in a completely different light.

The importance of running for extended periods of time

Is running still really helpful and recommended in modern soccer?

I can imagine it may frighten inexperienced coaches but:
- when properly measured out, running is much less dangerous than hops, for instance, specifically when they are performed in abundance by players who have never practiced them and can not do them properly;
- running is useful and irreplaceable in some particular situations. As to the importance of running in some particular situations, in

my book 'Soccer: The Present and the Future' and in the technical magazine published by the Italian soccer association - I have stated that running can be particularly helpful from these points of view (see table 14.1):

- in the warm up phase; a few laps around the playing field suffice to raise the body temperature and to bring about some of the physical adaptations at which the warm up is specifically aimed;
- in the warm down period at the end of the training session or at the end of the match, if necessary; running is also recommended and helpful in the morning session immediately following the match;
- as a conditioning method for favoring the balance in the body temperature, specifically when players know they are going to play in completely different weather conditions (higher temperature, relative humidity and sun radiation levels than those they were accustomed to). This problem was discussed in detail in paragraph 13.5;
- as a method for favoring slimming down in players whose body fat concentrations are particularly high, but only if it is combined with a suitable diet;
- to prepare the body to endure heavier workloads (that is as a sort of 'training for training' or 'athletic conditioning preparing the body for real training' - as I have already defined it thousands of times, at least!) specifically when recovering from a pause due to holiday, injury, illness or other reasons.

To amateur soccer players who have not performed any kind of physical activity at all for about two months I would suggest the same conditioning method to start their pre-season which I suggested to professional athletes 15 or 20 years ago. The very first training sessions should begin with a few minutes' running on level ground. Day by day, the exercise should become increasingly demanding: for instance, it could include ups and downs, speed variations, sprints and be protracted for increasingly long periods of time. I am sure that - after a total of 40 to 50 kilometers covered in about 4 hours or even more in 8 to 10 training sessions - players would experience several changes and physical adaptations, in particular their capacities to endure heavier workloads and fatigue would be significantly enhanced.

In chapter twelve (in paragraph 12.2, in particular), I already

Purpose	Function	Workloads
re-education	increase the capacities to work and endure exercise (prepare the body to real training)	Increasingly long distance, up to 8 kilometers and even more
warm-up	prepare the body to training or to the match	from 1 to 3 km
post-match exercise	help the body to recover from fatigue immediately after the match or the next day	up to 2 km (immediately after the match) or up to 5 or 6 km (the next day)
regulate the body temperature	help the body to acclimate to unusual weather conditions	Increasingly long distances up to 8 km and even more
slimming down	help to reduce excess fat	km per training session at least (combined to a proper diet)

Table 14.1
The main situations where running can be useful and highly recommended.

pointed out that, if on one hand it is true that a certain ability can be seriously impaired if that quality is not thoroughly trained for a certain period of time, on the other side it is also true that when a particular exercise negatively affects certain physical attributes, it is fundamental for players to perform specific workouts to counterbalance those negative effects. This is valid also for running, specifically when it is protracted for significant periods of time, like several minutes in one single session or for a few hours during the course of the same week.

Endurance Training In Junior and Senior Athletes

Conditioning methods and workloads will vary in relation to age. In general, the younger the player, the more specific endurance training should be suggested as a game; the younger the player, the less frequent the conditioning sessions specifically focused on training the various components of endurance should be. As to the over 30 year olds, in general there are no contraindications or problems of any kind concerning endurance training for this age group.

Training the aerobic components of endurance in youth players

In those individuals who have never performed specific endurance training, maximal oxygen consumption - also when it is expressed as an absolute value (that is in liters of oxygen per minute) - reaches its maximum values at about the age of 17. Furthermore, when it is expressed in relation to the body weight (that is in milliliters of oxygen per kilogram of body weight and per minute), it reaches its peak values much earlier, at about the age of 10 to 13. Considering the reality from this point of view, there would be no physiological problems which advise against suggesting specific exercise involving the activation of anaerobic mechanisms to young athletes. The real problems would be mainly psychological (since youths - until a certain age, at least - often fail to endure high-intensity performances for a long time) and of other nature (in particular, concerning the priority given to the choices of the qualities and skills one wants to enhance in that period of time, which is often extremely short).

At what age is it advisable to begin to regularly train the aerobic components of endurance in young soccer players?

Many years ago, I happened to read the results of an American research carried out on a number of couples of monozygotic twins, that is twins who develop from the two halves of a single egg and therefore look almost alike and have the same genetic material. One of the two twins was subjected to specific endurance training, even though it was rather light exercise. The other, by contrast, did nothing more than his usual school and leisure physical activities. Obviously, the former experienced a much more significant improvement in aerobic tests then his twin. However, if specific endurance conditioning was suggested before the age of maximal height growth - that is the period when standing height experiences a sudden increase, whose peak is between the age of 13 and 15, in general - basic aerobic features no longer differed from one twin to the other after that particular age, as if specific exercise previously carried out by the first twin had been completely useless. Another research, a Japanese study this time, seemed to draw different conclusions. In particular, it proved that specific endurance training can be helpful also when it is performed before the age of maximal height growth, if it involves sufficiently hard workloads and significant physical effort (like in the case of very young middle-distance runners' athletic conditioning).

Those publications together with my personal experiences have gradually induced me to believe that, in practice, under 14 year old soccer players cannot really benefit so much from specific training for the aerobic components of endurance (but I am always ready to change my mind if something new emerges which proves the contrary is true). In any case, it could be helpful to plan various team games like those which G. Vanni suggests. By contrast, after the age of 14, young soccer players should practice specific endurance conditioning. It is important to thoroughly plan specific workouts to avoid too heavy workloads; one single specific endurance session a month would suffice at the very beginning, and could be based on a few team games involving prolonged running; in particular, it should include speed variations and could also combine muscular exercise (like hurdling, slalom running, hops, skips and so forth...) and/or practice with the ball. In 1992, prof. Pincolini (Arrigo Sacchi's fitness coach) said: "*The ability to run in different ways, in the most proper and accurate manner, either with or without the ball, slowly and steadily for a time or in sudden short sprints, should gradually become something automatic. Only in this way, can very young soccer players perfectly internalize a movement which is both basic and fundamental and extremely different in the various phases of a match*".

Starting from the age of 16, the aerobic components of endurance can be trained much more accurately and specifically. In 1992, prof. Pincolini stated: "*I think that an increasingly specific and well-aimed periodization of athletic conditioning would be of critical importance between the ages of 16 and 20. I think that, in the months of December, January and February - while always considering the possible problems resulting from those particular weather conditions - the coach should plan specific periods of heavy physical exercise, combining general strengthening and the development of both aerobic endurance - which is fundamental in this age group, in my opinion - and anaerobic capacities*".

From the age of 16 on, not only is it possible to train the aerobic components of endurance, but it is also necessary to enhance those capacities. My personal experience has gradually helped me to realize that significant improvements can be brought about by specific endurance training in this age group. For instance, the anaerobic threshold rises so rapidly that even those youths who could not endure prolonged running at the beginning of the conditioning period, can gradually improve and achieve important results after good pre-season training and after aerobic exercise or similar workouts regularly carried out every week (in particular, some of them can even run 3,300 meters in the Cooper test or run 1,000 meter repetitions in less than 3 minutes 20 seconds). What is really important is that those physical adaptations and significant improvements appear to be permanent, in the sense that many of those players will always belong to the category of good runners capable of physical endurance. Obviously, they will be able to further enhance their aerobic capacities if they are lucky enough to play for teams where such qualities are thoroughly trained.

In conclusion, I believe that, between the ages of 16 and 18 (and still more between the ages of 18 and 20), one training session a week should be mainly dedicated to specific exercise for the aerobic components of endurance - the peripheral ones, in particular. I am convinced that, from this point of view, an 18 or 19 year old player should be considered as a 22 or 25 year old, even though athletic conditioning must be accurately planned in relation to the qualities and capacities of every single player.

As to the central aerobic components of endurance, again I think that it is useless to differentiate between 17 to 18 year olds and 22 to 25 year olds - specifically during the pre-season conditioning period - while I believe the coach should be particularly careful when addressing 15 to 16 year old players.

Training the lactic acid components of endurance in youth players

In the previous paragraph, I pointed out that the aerobic components of endurance - measured in values of maximal oxygen consumption - are well-developed at a very young age and even in those who have never done anything at all to enhance them. By contrast, the reality is completely different for the lactic acid components of endurance, since they are poorly developed in very young individuals.

The capacity of muscles to produce ATP through the lactic acid mechanism and their capacity to endure the consequent variations in blood acidity and lactate concentration are also directly connected to some particular enzymes, whose concentration varies in relation to age: the younger the individual, the lower the concentration of those enzymes.

This means that youths cannot endure lactic acid exercise, and this is particularly evident in young soccer players under the age of 16. From that age on, youths can gradually experience a significant improvement of their lactic acid capacities.

This is why I recommend that coaches begin to thoroughly train the lactic acid components once a week starting from the age of 16, alternating a lactic acid activity with the ball with lactic acid exercise without the ball, if necessary. In this age group I would suggest that coaches give the priority to those workouts which also enhance lactic acid power, that is those activities which were classified as 2.1, 2.2 and 2.3 in paragraph 9.2 in chapter nine.

In conclusion, and I am perfectly aware that many people completely disagree with what I am going to say, the coach should make no difference between specific training for the lactic acid components of endurance in 17 to 18 year olds and specific endurance conditioning for four or eight year older players (as was previously said for the aerobic components).

Endurance training in 'older' players

The over 30 year olds are usually considered 'elderly players' in soccer. Should they take any particular precaution when performing specific endurance training?

For other types of physical exercise (hops, in particular), 'senior' players should sometimes be considered 'at risk': for instance, an over 30 year old player who has never made hops or cannot hop properly or has been prone to injuries to his lower limbs during the course of his soccer career, is obviously very likely to suffer from traumatic disorders specifically affecting the knees and Achilles tendons, since they are particularly subject to stresses.

As to running, on the contrary, a 22 year old athlete is as vulnerable to injuries as a 26 year old. In short, this factor alone cannot limit specific endurance conditioning in over 30 year old soccer players.

Furthermore, if we consider the reality from another point of view - that is from the possibility of enhancing the various components of endurance - we should immediately underline that there are no problems at all as to aerobic components. Not only can they be maintained at maximum levels in 'old athletes', but they can also be further improved if specific endurance training is thoroughly planned both at quantitative and qualitative level. In those sports where ATP is mostly produced by the aerobic mechanism - like in marathon racing, cross-country skiing or cycling - many athletes are able to achieve their best results and show their best performances at about the age of 35 or even more.

The same is not true for the lactic acid components of endurance, in the sense that maximum capacities and performances in those where such components are of critical importance generally begin to decrease gradually after the age of 30. According to my personal experience, this gradual depletion can be easily reduced in 'senior' soccer players. Furthermore, there could even be an improvement in lactic acid components in those who have never trained them thoroughly. In short, there are no sound reasons for suggesting different aerobic or lactic acid training plans to 'old' athletes from 22 or 25 year olds, although it is always fundamental to carefully monitor their personal reactions to some specific workouts, those for lactic acid and central aerobic components of endurance in particular.

The fact that this paragraph specifically focuses on 'senior' athletes also gives me the opportunity for pointing out that - unlike what some firmly believe - it is absolutely wrong that those who usually run a lot during training sessions and matches generally have much shorter careers than those who practice less and are therefore less efficient in their athletic performances. Certainly, those who have innate marked technical skills can easily maintain them after the age of 30 and are therefore more likely to find clubs which still need their performances in spite of their age. Nevertheless, my personal experience has gradually helped me to realize that those who have not such natural technical skills but have progressively enhanced their endurance capacities by means of constant training throughout the years, are usually highly appreciated and can work to maintain them at high levels far beyond the age of 30, provided that they regularly train such capacities.

16

Conclusions

I began a few years ago to collect all the information and material I needed to write this book. I intended to achieve two important goals: I did not want to leave out something important (at least, I did not want to neglect those aspects which I consider important for those who will read this book) and, above all, I resolved to be as clear as possible and explain basic important concepts in an easy-to-read manner.

I do not intend to persuade everybody to accept my training methods and plan athletic conditioning according to my personal ideas. I would simply like to teach some coaches and fitness coaches a new method for dealing with the main problems of soccer training, while also trying 'to get into the human body' to try to understand how it really works and then study how it can be modified - by means of constant training - to bring about better performances. For this to be possible, it is fundamental to combine theoretical knowledge resulting from scientific research with one's personal experience directly on the field.

As far as scientific research is concerned, I would like to clearly specify that my intent was to write a book which could act as a practical reference in soccer, to help coaches and fitness coaches to train the various components of endurance in a more specific and suitable manner.

Appendices

Field tests to evaluate aerobic fitness (endurance)

Among all the possible field tests to evaluate some of the components of endurance in soccer players, we would like to specifically focus the attention on:

- Cooper Test and one of its possible variations;
- 3,000 meter distance (paragraph A.1);
- Conconi and Sassi Test (paragraph A.2);
- Probst Test (paragraph A.3);
- LÈger Test (paragraph A.4);
- Capanna and Sassi shuttle run test (paragraph A.5).

There are several other testing methods which have been used (and are currently used) in soccer; the five tests which we are going to deal with are particularly advantageous, since they are 'field tests', are cheap and simple to perform, do not require complex equipment (a stop watch, a cardio-meter, a recorded beeps device, that is a specific device uttering regular beeps at set intervals of time and which can also be incorporated in the cardio-meter itself) and can be run by the coach or the fitness coach.

A.1 Cooper Test

This field test is extremely simple to perform: it simply involves running for a set time (12 minutes) and the distance covered being recorded. It was set up by Kenneth H. Cooper, who was a NASA physician at that time and then founder of those institutes specifically designed for studying both aerobic exercise and the individuals performing aerobic activities. The Cooper Test can help to assess the differences in endurance aerobic features of individuals belonging to very heterogeneous target groups, like a group of recruits or the students of a whole school. It can be very useful in soccer too, since the capacity to run over a considerable distance in 12 minutes certainly indicates that the athlete is particularly efficient from the aerobic point of view: in short, physical effort being equal, the player who can run 3,400 meters in 12 minutes obviously has a higher maximal oxygen uptake and is more capable of aerobic endurance than a fellow athlete who can run only 2,600 meters in the same interval of time.

Development - Players run along a 400 meter track and field oval or along an accurately measured path on level ground (an oval track around the playing field, for instance). After proper warm up (which could include 8 to 10 minutes stretch, a few minutes running and some short sprints, for example), players start all together, or, better, in groups of 10 to 12 individuals at a time, at most. The coach should previously advise them on the importance of running at a constant pace, which best suits their personal features. He should also tell them the times they are running at set distances (for instance, at the very first 200 and 400 meters and when covering each kilometer) or clearly announce them if they are either early or late according to suitable norm tables setting specific running times in relation to particular physical attributes. Players should always know how much time has elapsed and/or how much time is left. As soon as the stop watch strikes twelve minutes, the coach gives the signal (by blowing his whistle, for example): all the players stop on the spot and leave a mark to identify their positions.

Scoring - The accurate distance covered by every single player can be properly measured by referring to the number of laps and to some set marks along the track (those marked on the curb of the track every 50 or 100 meters, for instance), and then carefully measuring the distance between those marks and the spot where each athlete stopped. There is a standard table (table A.1) which helps to assess the distance covered in 12 minutes through a list of adjectives (this is therefore a rather rough manner to evaluate the performance). In my opinion, it is rather useless to refer to that table in soccer.

However, the distance athletes can cover in 12 minutes can be used to measure their average running speed in Km/h. This is possible by simply multiplying the total distance covered in kilometers and fractions of kilometers by 5. For instance, a player who runs 3 kilometers 120 meters (= 3.120 Km) has an average running speed of 15.600 Km/h (since 3.120 x 5 = 15.600). Soccer players' average running speed over 12 minutes is generally close to (or a little faster than) their anaerobic threshold pace. Remember that a middle-distance or long-distance runner in track and field can usually maintain a speed which is 15% faster than his anaerobic threshold pace over 12 minutes. By contrast, due to their poor psychological disposition to endure constant high-intensity exercise for several minutes, soccer players generally fail to maintain that speed for even shorter periods of time.

Distance covered in 12 minutes	Scoring
less than 1,600 meters	very poor
from 1,600 to 2,000 meters	poor
from 2,000 to 2,400 meters	low average
from 2,400 to 2,800 meters	high average
from 2,800 to 3,200 meter	very poor
more than 3,200 meters	excellent

Table A.1
Norm table set up by Kenneth H. Cooper himself to assess the distance covered in the Cooper Test. It can be used when testing groups of recruits or senior high school students; it seems to be rather useless in soccer.

Shifting from the distance covered in 12 minutes to the choice of suitable training rhythms - Apart from monitoring and assessing the progress or the decline occurring over a certain interval of time (from the end of the previous season to the beginning of the following one, or throughout the pre-season training period, for example), the Cooper Test can also help to evaluate the most suitable pace each athlete should maintain while running aerobic repetitions. Table 6.3 (in chapter six) can be used to assess the times for players to run 1,000 meter repetitions, while table 6.5 can help to set the times for 500 , 600 and 800 meter running repetitions.

3,000 meter run Test - From the practical point of view, it is sometimes much simpler and more convenient to replace the standard Cooper test with another similar field test involving running for a set distance (3,000 meters, in particular) and time required being recorded. Timing the athlete's performance over a set distance definitely helps the coach to better assess every single player's perfor mance capabilities. Table 6.4 allows to set the times for 1,000 meter running repetitions specifically aimed at enhancing peripheral aerobic components of endurance, depending on the times required for covering a 3,000 meter distance.

A.2 Conconi and Sassi Test

The Conconi Test was set up in the mid 70s and was first addressed to runners and race walkers. As time went by, it was also applied to other sports disciplines. It was devised by Francesco Conconi, who immediately proposed it as an instrument for assessing athletes' capabilities. Later on, other people gradually began to suggest this field test as a method for properly selecting the rhythms of training. Conconi Test was first introduced in soccer by Roberto Sassi, who made various adjustments to the standard testing method. In particular, he began to conduct the Conconi test directly on the playing field and also started to collect and process data and statistical information about players' heart rates after performing the test. Sassi also offered important suggestions as to the practical use of the test.

Development - For the test to be performed properly, the player must first of all wear a highly reliable cardio-meter. After suitable warm up, the analyzed athlete runs a few kilometers along the track and field oval or along the path which Sassi suggests for soccer players, maybe a well-marked running track around the playing field (see diagram A.1): the athlete runs along the two long sides of the field, rounding off the corners of the pitch while also passing behind the goals, if possible.

The running speed should be very low at the beginning (8 to 10 kilometers an hour); then, it rises gradually, by about 0.5 Km/h every basic segment accounting for:

- about 200 meters in a track and field oval (which is 400 meters long);
- half a lap in an oval running track marked around the playing field and passing behind the two goals;
- one whole lap if the oval track around the field is shorter than 250 to 280 meters.

While running the first 20 meters of every basic segment, the athlete's running speed should increase slightly, while it should be as constant as possible while running the remaining part of each basic segment (diagram A1). In the precise instant when each basic segment ends, the player reads his heart rate displayed on the cardio-meter he is wearing and promptly communicates it to the fitness coach and his fellow coaches, who are also responsible for timing the athlete's performance and writing down the times it takes for him to run each basic segment. If the athlete is wearing a cardio-meter which automatically records and displays both the time and his heart rate, he only needs to press the specific button when passing each basic segment. In order to draw out an accurate graph, the

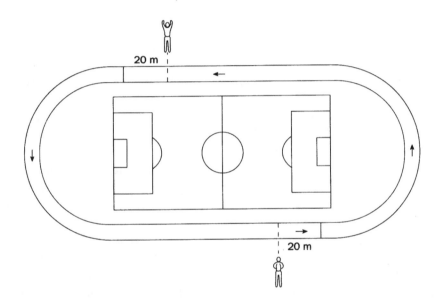

Diagram A.1 - The diagram shows how the Conconi and Sassi Test can be performed along a standard track and field oval or along an oval track previously marked out around the playing field, passing behind the two goals. The running track is divided in two halves (basic segments); at the end of each basic segment, the fitness coach and another coach accurately record the time it takes for the athlete to cover that distance and the heart rate that the player reads on his cardio-meter display and communicates to them; when using specific modern cardio-meters, the athlete only needs to press the button which automatically records both the time required and the heart rate when he completes each basic segment. While running the first 20 meters of each basic segment, the athlete promptly increases his running speed and he tries to keep his pace as constant as possible while running the remaining part of each basic segment.

running track should be divided into 12 to 16 basic segments, corresponding to 6 to 8 laps around a standard track and field oval, and to 12 to 16 laps along a shorter oval track. Today, some modern cardio-meters include specific devices uttering regular acoustic signals, which therefore help the athlete to easily maintain his pace and gradually increase his running speed properly. In this way, the testing method is much more reliable and this also allows the coach to carefully compare the tests performed by different athletes or by the same athlete in different periods.

Scoring - The graph in diagram A.2 shows heart rate values to running speed. Some modern cardio-meters now allow you to immediately enter the data collected in computers, which promptly process them by means of specific programs, and directly draw up the graph we need.

The line combining the various points in the graph at first has a straight development, since the athlete's heart rate rises steadily as his running speed increases. However, at a certain running speed the development is no longer linear, since the heart rate begins to rise less than before. This particular running speed (that is the point where the straight line turns to be a curved line) is defined as 'deflection speed' and is generally very close to the individual's anaerobic threshold pace.

Furthermore, the heart rate at rest is subtracted from the heart rate during recovery intervals (measured after 15, 45, 75, 105 and 135 seconds); the figures one gets from that subtraction are then expressed in function to the logarithm of the time required. The result is a straight line which indicates the time that it takes for the heart rate to reduce by half during the recovery phase. As the athlete gradually improves his fitness condition, his heart rate lowers more rapidly and, consequently, the inclination of the line changes.

Advantages and limits of the Conconi and Sassi Test - The Conconi and Sassi Test can therefore be used to evaluate some important capabilities of soccer players. In particular, it allows us to measure a player's anaerobic threshold, from which it is possible to set the ideal speed that every athlete should maintain in specific running styles (see table 6.2 in chapter six). This test can also help to compare the data collected in various periods throughout the soccer season and therefore assess the rise and the decline of some particular values, such as the deflection speed, the straight line in the test graph and the line indicating the athlete's heart recovery.

· Remember that, in 1991 prof. Bosco pointed out that 4 authors had proven that there cannot always be a direct correlation between the deflection in the Conconi Test and the athlete's anaerobic threshold measured in relation to his blood lactate concentration, another 4 authors had stated that such deflection is not always present, and 3 authors had declared that the estimate of the deflection point is subjective and therefore depends on the recorder's personal interpretation. Nevertheless, the Conconi and Sassi Test can be very helpful for coaches who directly work on the playing field, specifically when it is scheduled at regular intervals of time. As to the very early stage in this testing method, there are no particular problems when drawing the straight line (even though we cannot really speak of the Conconi test if we only consider this part of the graph - as somebody has reasonably pointed out). If the straight line turns to the right - which means lower heart rate values, running speed being equal - this indicates an improvement in the athlete's aerobic efficiency, while if it turns to the left, this suggests a depletion in the athlete's aerobic fitness. Constantly repeating the test at regular intervals considerably helps to identify the exact deflection point, at least because the deflection heart rate in the same individual either changes very slowly in time or remains constant for several years.

Diagram A.2
Computer graphics development ml/Kg/min of Conconi and Sassi Test; the abscissa indicates the athlete's running speed (Km/h), while the ordinate represents the heart rate (heart beats per minute). Up to a certain running speed, the points in the graph position so as to grow steadily and form a straight line (when the running speed rises, the heart rate also increases in the same proportion). But at a certain speed, which is defined as Ds minute (deflection speed), the points deflect and form a curve, whose concavity faces down; in this case, the deflection speed corresponds to 16.7 Km/h and to about 170 heart beats per minute. In short, the running speed rises steadily, while the heart rate increases less and more slowly than before.

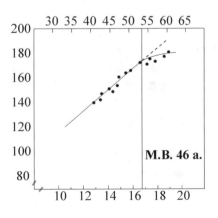

A.3 Probst Test

Both the Cooper Test and the Conconi and Sassi test are specifically aimed at assessing the player's aerobic capacities while he is running along a straight path or a curved track. The Swiss physician Hans Peter Probst rightly observed that those testing methods did not consider that the athlete's running direction constantly changes in soccer, and involves several muscle groups which do not generally work at all in straight running. This is why he conceived (together with Daniel Jeandupeauz, a very popular soccer coach, and other fellow volleyball and ice-hockey coaches) a specific field test in which athletes are asked to run a zig-zag course. Like in the Conconi and Sassi Test, the athlete is wearing a cardio-meter which constantly records his heart rate.

Development - The test can be performed directly on the playing field. Mark out a zig-zag circuit by positioning 14 flag posts or flat marker cones 10 meters apart in a 20 by 48 yards rectangular area, like in diagram A.3. The track is 140 meters long and must be performed twice (which means a distance of 280 meters, in total) with no pauses in-between, at a certain running speed - it is quite easy for the player to maintain a constant pace, since he knows he has to be near one of the flag posts whenever he hears the acoustic signal. Several players can perform the test simultaneously (depending on the number of cardio-meters available at the moment), starting at a certain distance from each other (one or a few flag posts apart).

    The players start the test running two laps at a speed of 10.8 Km/h, which means that the coach gives 18 acoustic signals per minute. Then, after a 30 seconds' recovery interval (it is possible to take blood samples during that interval, to measure players' blood lactate concentrations), the athletes run another two laps at a slightly faster speed (+ 0.6 Km/h). After another 30 seconds' pause, they promptly restart and perform the zig-zag circuit twice again at a still faster running pace. The speed increases gradually until the player can no longer endure the rhythm (table A.2).

Scoring - The average heart rate values of each player over the last 15 seconds in every double circuit are introduced in the graph in relation to his running speed (see diagram A.4). Like in the Conconi and Sassi Test, these heart rate values first develop and form a straight line. However, when the athlete is approaching his anaerobic threshold, such values no longer rise at the same rhythm as

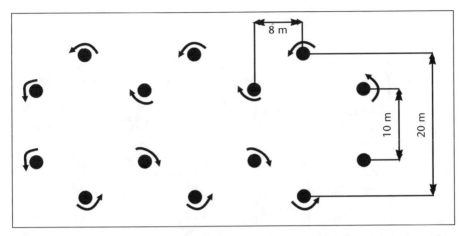

Diagram A.3 - The zig-zag circuit in the Probst Test; the track is marked out by placing 14 flag posts or marker cones in a 20 by 48 yards playing area. One lap corresponds to 140 meters.

before and the line deflects to form a curve. According to Probst's statistical parameters, the higher the level of player performing the test, the more the deflection speed measured in this way is similar to the deflection speed in the Conconi and Sassi test. This means that professional players (in the Italian Serie A, for instance) have very similar deflection speeds in both tests, while athletes playing in lower divisions (in the Italian Serie C, for example) already show significant differences (obviously, the deflection speed is slower in the Probst Test). Such differences become still more evident in amateur players. Maximum differences are usually recorded in track and field runners, since they are not used to changing their running directions; furthermore, some of them are even obliged to interrupt the test due to muscle pain.

A.4 LÈger Test

This test was set up by prof. Luc LÈger and his team at Montreal University. Prof. Marella first introduced and applied this test in Italy, while also introducing an important variation to the standard testing method: the athlete is wearing a cardio-meter while performing the test, so that his heart rate values are carefully recorded during the performance and finally entered in computer diagrams.

Development - The test requires the athlete to run back and forth ('shuttle run') along a 20 meter-long track as long as possible, at a set speed which is steadily imposed from the outside: an acoustic

Repetition	Speed km/h	Total Time (required sec)	Partial Time (required sec)
1	10.80	93.33	3.33
2	11.40	88.42	3.16
3	12.00	84.00	3.00
4	12.60	80.00	2.86
5	13.20	76.36	2.73
6	13.80	73.04	2.61
7	14.40	70.00	2.50
8	15.00	67.20	2.40
9	15.60	64.62	2.31
10	16.20	62.22	2.22
11	16.80	60.00	2.14
12	17.40	57.43	2.07
13	18.00	56.00	2.00
14	18.60	54.19	1.94
15	19.20	52.50	1.88
16	19.80	50.91	1.82
17	20.40	49.41	1.76

Table A.2

If the cardio-meter does not include an acoustic timer, the Probst Test can only be performed if the player is properly signaled (by means of a whistle, for instance) the moment when he should be near one of the various cones. For each repetition (which corresponds to two laps in the zig-zag circuit, that is 280 meters), this table shows: the running speed (in Km/h), the total time.

Velocity (km/h)	Average Heart Rate
• 10.80	150
11.40	154
12.00	159
12.60	163
13.20	167
13.80	174
14.40	176
• 15.00	180
15.60	183
16.20	186
16.80	189

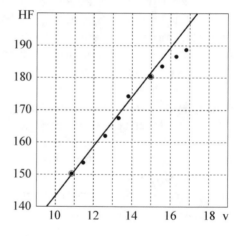

Diagram A.4 - Development of the heart required for each repetition (in seconds) and in relation to the athlete's running speed; the interval of time which it should take for the point where the straight line deflects the athlete to move between two consecutive ('deflection speed') corresponds to 15 cones, according to standard testing protocols. Km/h, in this case, and also corresponds to the athlete's anaerobic threshold, in general (from Pilori, 1993).

signal constantly communicates to the player when he should be at one of the two ends of the track. Such running speed progressively increases every minute (see the proportions in table A.3). Several players can perform the test simultaneously, since each one can run along his own lane, whose ends are marked out by a line which needs to be touched with one foot or completely crossed. The performance ends when, for two consecutive times, the player can no longer reach one of the two ends of the track (or better: the spare area at the 18th meter) when the signal is uttered.

Scoring - Table A.3 (the second column from the right) clearly gives us an idea of the values of maximal oxygen uptake (VO2 max) in relation to the duration of the test. In the first column on the right, I have tried to suggest the times recommended for 1,000 meter running repetitions, when the exercise is specifically aimed at enhancing the peripheral aerobic components of endurance; obviously, there may be significant differences from an athlete to another.

A.5 Capanna and Sassi shuttle run test

The shuttle run test was conceived by Riccardo Capanna and Roberto Sassi. This test requires the athlete to run six times back and forth along a 40 meter-long track. The player starts from a standing position and promptly turns around after the first 20 meters to change his running direction. The recovery interval between two consecutive trials is 20 seconds. For a long time, soccer players' running speeds have been measured by timing their performances over distances of 10 to 50 or 60 meters or even more; this shuttle run test not only lets us assess the athlete's sprinting skills (that is his capacity to build up speed in a very short space), but - if one only limits to timing the first performance - it also helps to evaluate other attributes of critical importance in soccer, like the ability to slow down, turn around and promptly speed up in a very short time. And, above all, the test as a whole finally lets us assess the athlete's resistance to sprint. While running the first shuttle, muscles mostly use up stored ATP and phosphocreatine; during the recovery interval, they re-synthesize part of those high-energy phosphates - the higher the capacity to replace non-lactic acid oxygen debt, the larger the amount of phosphates they can re-synthesize. In the following trials, an increasingly small amount of phosphocreatine is available and can be used by working muscles; consequently, a larger quantity of lactic acid is produced and therefore stores in muscle fibers.

Time (max)	Speed (km/h)	Time over 20 m. (sec.)	VO2 max (ml/kg/min)	1000 m. (min. and sec.)
2	7.51	9.693	24.5	-
4	8.70	8.276	31.5	-
6	9.30	7.744	35.0	5'10"-5'15"
8	9.90	7.276	38.5	4'55"- 5'00"
10	10.49	6.862	42.0	4'30' - 4'35"
12	11.09	6.492	45.5	4'10" - 4'15"
14	11.69	6.160	49.0	3'52" - 3'57"
16	12.29	5.860	52.5	3'37" - 3'42"
18	12.88	5.589	56.0	3'23" - 3'28"
20	13.48	5.341	59.5	3'11" - 3'16"
22	14.08	5.114	63.0	3'00" - 3'05"
24	14.68	4.906	66.5	2'51" - 2'56"
26	15.27	4.714	70.0	2'43" - 2'48"
28	15.87	4.537	73.5	2'35" - 2'40"
30	16.47	4.372	77.0	-

Table A.3
Depending on the time (first column) for which the player is able to keep up with the running speed stressed by the beeper device, the table suggests: maximum speed (expressed in kilometers per hour), the time required for running each 20 meter repetition (in seconds), maximal oxygen uptake (in milliliters per kilogram of body weight per minute) and a rough estimate of the time it would take for the athlete to run 1,000 meter aerobic repetitions when the exercise is specifically aimed at enhancing the peripheral aerobic components of endurance.

Development - As explained before, the test involves the player to run 6 times back and forth along a 20 meter straight track between two parallel lines marked out on the playing field in the shortest time possible. Obviously, this requires the player to promptly turn around and change his running direction, since he first runs forward and then runs back in the opposite direction. It is fundamental to accurately measure the distance; the athlete must cover the whole distance and cannot turn around before reaching the farthest point of the track (for instance, he can be asked either to touch the 20 meter line or cross it with one foot, or to touch or pick up something on the line). The most important thing is to maintain the same rules to properly compare the results. The performance can be perfectly timed by means of suitable photocells or specific platforms; however, as Sassi pointed out in 1991, it is also possible to time the trial manually without this being detrimental to the final result of the test. The recovery interval between two consecutive 40 meter shuttle repetitions is 20 seconds.

Scoring - As underlined in the previous paragraph, the athlete's sprinting skills can be properly assessed in relation to the time required to run the first repetition, since the symptoms of fatigue cannot generally appear in that first period. Fatigue obviously impairs the athlete's performance, so that the time required to cover the same distance gradually tends to worsen: the greater the player's 'resistance to sprint', the more the times required in the last repetitions will be similar to those in the first trials.

When drawing up a graph like that in diagram A.5, it is possible to draw a straight line either by hand or by using specific computer programs, like those which Roberto Sassi suggests; the slope of that line indicates the player's resistance: the slighter the slope (which means: the less it rises from the first to the fifth trial - that is from the left to the right of the graph), the greater the player's resistance.

A much simpler way for assessing the player's resistance to sprint is to measure the difference between the time required in the first two shuttles and the time required in the last two repetitions.

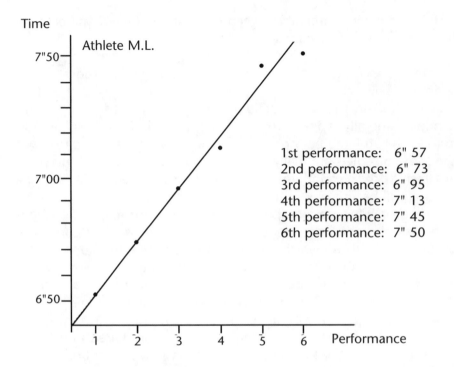

Diagram A.5 - Graph of The Capanna and Sassi shuttle run test performed by a soccer player (M.L.) with times of 6' 51, 6' 73, 6' 95, 7'13, 7' 45 and 7' 50 respectively in the six performances. In this case, there is a significant depletion in the athleteís performance while passing from the first to the six trial.

Coaching Books from REEDSWAIN

#785:
The Complete Book
of
Soccer Restart Plays
by Mario Bonfanti and
Angelo Pereni
$14.95

#154:
Coaching Soccer
by Bert van Lingen
$14.95

#177:
PRINCIPLES OF
Brazilian Soccer
by José Thadeu
Goncalves
in cooperation with Prof. Julio Mazzei
$16.95

#185:
Conditioning
for Soccer
Dr. Raymond Verheijen
$19.95

#244:
Coaching the 4-4-2
by Maziali and Mora
$14.95

#787:
Attacking Schemes
and Training
Exercises
by Eugenio Fascetti and
Romedio Scaia
$14.95

Call REEDSWAIN 1-800-331-5191

Coaching Books from REEDSWAIN

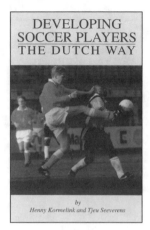

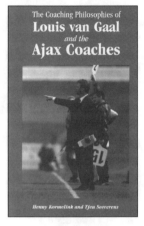

#786:
Soccer
Nutrition
by Enrico Arcelli
$10.95

#267:
Developing
Soccer Players
THE DUTCH WAY
$12.95

#175:
The Coaching Philosophies of
Louis van Gaal
and the
Ajax Coaches
by Kormelink and
Seeverens
$14.95

#284:
The Dutch Coaching
Notebook
$14.95

#287:
Team Building
by Kormelink
and Seeverens
$9.95

#788:
Zone Play
by Pereni and di Cesare
$14.95

Web Site: www.reedswain.com

Notes

REEDSWAIN BOOKS and VIDEOS
1-800-331-5191 • www.reedswain.com

Notes

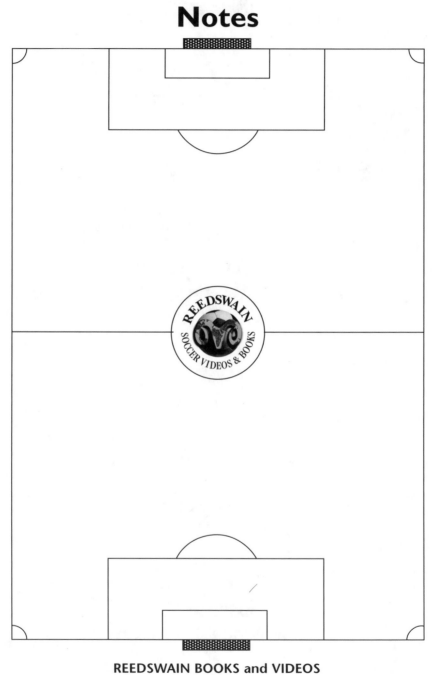

REEDSWAIN BOOKS and VIDEOS
1-800-331-5191 • www.reedswain.com